FAMILY TIME

CONTENTS

REMINISCE

EXECUTIVE EDITOR Kirsten Schrader
ASSOCIATE CREATIVE DIRECTOR
Christina Spalatin
DEPUTY EDITOR Mary-Liz Shaw
ART DIRECTOR Kristen Stecklein
ASSOCIATE EDITOR Julie Kuczynski
COPY EDITOR Sara Strauss
PRODUCTION COORDINATOR
Jon Syverson
SENIOR RIGHTS ASSOCIATE
Jill Godsey

PICTURED ON FRONT COVER
Family and pool,
Lambert/Getty Images

COLORIZATION
Sanna Dullaway

ADDITIONAL PHOTO CREDITS
Color paper backgrounds:
Ekaterina Romanova/Getty Images;
ExpressIPhoto/Getty Images
Square frames:
Eileen Mattison; Robert Steams

© 2020 RDA Enthusiast Brands, LLC.
1610 N. 2nd St., Suite 102
Milwaukee, WI 53212-3906

International Standard Book Number:
978-1-61765-986-7
Library of Congress Control Number:
2020936335
Component Number:
117300100H

All rights reserved.
Printed in U.S.A.
1 3 5 7 9 10 8 6 4 2

A SPECIAL KIND OF BOND

These are the memories of those who recall the joy of family — the time they took a cross-country road trip in the new car, spent an afternoon at the ballpark with Dad or took in a lazy round of mini-golf on a hot summer day with the whole gang.

A favorite in this collection, though short, is a memory of spending summers with Grandma. The recollection from contributor Lorraine Shank (page 167) is enough for many of us to think back on watching trees bend in the wind from a porch swing, smelling treats baking in an oven, and tasting sweet lemonade or, as in this story, homemade root beer. Lorraine would wake up on the Fourth of July to make the beverage with her grandmother. Afterward, they would go to watch fireworks in the evening.

We hope you relate to the cherished memories within *Family Time*. The book is sure to spark conversation with loved ones.

The Editors of *Reminisce* Magazine

Miniature golf has always been an activity for the whole family to enjoy — colorful outfits are optional.

RELATIVE AMUSEMENTS

Story time, board games, winter sports and summer picnics — some
activities are always more fun when we do them together.

Wait Your Turn

Brother shared his toys but made her stand by for the comic books.

My brother Fred was 18 months older than me. Whatever interested him interested me, too. He didn't like it, but our parents insisted that he share his toys with me. I loved playing with his Lionel train set and building windmills and skyscrapers with his Erector Set.

But the sharing rule was different for comic books: There was an unwritten law that whoever had the comic books was allowed to keep them until they'd finished reading what they chose.

We always had a big tug-of-war over *Batman* and *Superman*. Luckily, sharing was not an issue when it came to my favorites, like *Little Lulu* or *Little Lotta*, which Fred didn't like to read. And he wouldn't touch *Katy Keene*, which often came with paper dolls to cut out.

Fred would make a stack of his favorites and read them one by one, casting them aside as he finished. I waited patiently—sometimes—until he finished reading the whole pile, and then they were mine. I am convinced he tried to get away with reading as slowly as possible.

I've kept some of the *Katy Keene* comics, and they bring back memories of hours of quiet enjoyment that I didn't have to share with my big brother.

Judy Sikorski Rossford, OH

Judy watches in anticipation as her older brother Fred pores over his stack of Action Comics.

SMILES AT STORY TIME

Warm family moments gathered around a book inspire the joy of reading.

I especially loved the book *The Story of Ferdinand*. My father would do different voices for each character. Sometimes Dad would even create his own stories! He never failed to make us feel loved.
Lynn A. Ewing
Facebook

My mother was a librarian and helped instill in me a great love of reading. I passed that down to my daughters and try to do the same with my grandson. Books are friends that never leave you!
Mary Juba
Facebook

My dad used to sit with my siblings and me and read us all kinds of books. The one I remember most was *Green Eggs and Ham* by Dr. Seuss.
Beverly Duell-Moore
Facebook

Too Much Monkey Business

Competition between siblings can oftentimes be unfair.

Growing up in the 1950s and '60s with four siblings gave me many memorable experiences. Playing Monopoly with my two older brothers was just one of them.

Sitting at the kitchen table in our old farmhouse, my brothers taught me everything about board games that our parents didn't want us to know. When we played, Bruce (four years older than me) was the banker and Warren (seven years my elder) was the real estate agent. The cards were stacked against me from the start.

There was more cheating going on between the two of them than you'd find in a Hank Williams song. My brothers were sneaky, and they'd trade money and property cards under the table. When I wasn't looking, green houses and red hotels would magically appear on their properties. As the clock ticked, the boys got richer while I, their poor—very poor—and naive little sister, would get closer to bankruptcy.

After spending about an hour trying to prove they were cheating, I'd quit. Then I would exclaim that this was the last game of Monopoly I would ever play with them. Ever.

Inevitably, they would coax me to play again, promising no more monkey business. Over and over, I believed them. We would start another game, but just like a repeat of an old *Three Stooges* episode, the whole circus would start again.

So much for friendly competition. I still shake my head at what a gullible little sister I was!

Peggy Trowsdale Hadashville, MB

MONOPOLY LOVERS

These folks know why the game's been popular for decades.

Lesson Learned

Our Monopoly games could go on for a week or more. My mother, Rosa, had a special spot on the kitchen floor where we could keep the game board safe until the next day.

I'll always remember one game we kids played with my mom; my dad, Geoff; and a man named Pat, who worked for my dad. I was having an especially good game with hotels and houses on many properties, including Boardwalk and Park Place, so I spent a lot of time counting my money.

I noticed that everyone kept laughing. I realized, too late, that while I was counting my winnings, Pat had landed on my properties several times and moved on without paying me rent! If only Kenny Rogers' song "The Gambler" had been around then to instruct me—I didn't know not to count my money while sitting at the table!

Jean Skillman Wilsall, MT

Stashing Cash

My sister and I had a years-long "rivalry" over Monopoly. Every Saturday morning, we'd pull out the game and start to play. We used to hide money under the board and not tell the other one. So when we started to go bankrupt, we'd magically reach under and go, "Aha!" Then the game would continue.

Diane Dragan Facebook

Her and Scottie

My sister Eva and I played Monopoly every chance we got, but sometimes Eva would play only if I promised to bake a Chef Boyardee pizza from the box. I was more than happy to comply.

I loved the challenge of the game, and I loved buying hotels for all of my properties.

When either one of us ran out of play money, we would make up our own IOUs.

My favorite game piece? The cute little Scottie dog, of course!

Karin Rasmussen Grass Valley, CA

By the Kerosene Light

In the 1940s and '50s, my family always spent time each summer at a cabin in the pines near the town of Payson, Arizona.

At night we sat around the table lit by a kerosene lantern, playing Monopoly and eating dozens of my mom's chocolate chip cookies. I always bought the cheap properties so my money would go further, but then I'd end up going bankrupt when I landed on Boardwalk or Park Place.

Mary Ann Gove Phoenix, AZ

TRIPLE WORD THREAT

Daughters took after Mom with their fondness for playing Scrabble.

Born on a farm near Lester, Iowa, in 1907, my mother had—at most—a sixth-grade education, which she got in a one-room schoolhouse. She had to stop her formal schooling at a young age to help with the farm and to care for her mother, who was bedridden.

Yet Amelia Lauck Baumann was an amazing Scrabble player and a fierce competitor. She passed on her love of the game to my sister, Lorraine, and me.

While Lorraine and I don't live close to each other, whenever we are together, we have a Scrabble competition. Lorraine has been diagnosed with early onset dementia,

yet she has retained both her strong interest in and skill at playing Scrabble. Once we played a Scrabble series over almost three days, and Lorraine won nine games to my four.

We follow the rules strictly, although we do use a Scrabble dictionary from time to time. Over the years, we've learned a few tricks. Players often feel stumped when they get the X, Y or Z. But if you remember that many adjectives end in "y" and many adverbs in "ly," you can usually find a place on the board for Y.

The Z isn't much of a problem either, because of old standbys like "zoo," "zeal" and "zebra,"

plus there are several words that end in the letter, such as "topaz" and "waltz." The X can pose more of a problem, but it's not so bad if the board has an open A, E or O.

The problem letters for us are C and V. To the best of my knowledge, neither one of them can form a two-letter word.

The letter Q, however, can bring dread to the player who has it and doesn't also have a U. But a few years ago, I learned that "qi" is a word, so I don't fear the Q as much as I used to. If I'm lucky, I'll get the Z and the U, too, and hit the jackpot with "quiz."

Virgean Baumann Hazel Denver, CO

Winner for Life

My mother, Bertha Gates (right), and I loved playing Scrabble together. We played for hours and never got tired. Although I beat most players, Mother was as sharp as a tack. Even at age 95, she usually won.
Jane Bandy Vallejo, CA

RAUCOUS GAME NIGHTS

Every family has a favorite. Which was yours?

A little-known board game we loved was Shenanigans, put out after the TV show by the same name, starring Stubby Kaye. Very interactive and fun. Winter nights and rainy days always meant board games and popcorn — and we had plenty of both!

Kerry Trout Facebook

We played lots of board games growing up in the '50s. Candy Land and Chutes and Ladders were favorites. My sister, Margie, and I played Parcheesi almost every summer morning with our friend Candy on the picnic table in her backyard. We also liked Careers, Clue, Monopoly and Yahtzee. Today, my granddaughter, Brianna, plays Careers — we found it at a thrift store, since it's no longer made!

Mary Schmidt Facebook

Yahtzee! We still play board games with our grandchildren. We all especially like Yahtzee — it's great for the younger kids for math skills.

Marsha Ringo Burkes Facebook

The Big House

Fun was around every corner when staying at Grandma's place.

When I was in kindergarten in 1947, I moved into my Grandma Little's home with my mom and dad; my brother, Ronnie; and my sister, Patty. We called it the Big House. Perched on top of a hill in Glendale, California, and surrounded by a wide tree-lined avenue, it looked like a castle encircled by a moat. It was truly a child's paradise. Built in 1880, the home had four stories full of nooks and crannies—perfect small spaces for children to explore. The attic was a maze of boxes, old furniture and intriguing junk. I remember poring over old ledgers written in pen and pencil from the family trucking business.

The rooms were spacious and always filled with people. The family was huge—Grandma had 11 children—and there were always people coming and going. Most nights, everyone gathered in a back room off the kitchen that had a large oval table. It was not unusual for there to be 30 people seated for dinner.

We lived in the sunroom, a massive room jutting from the main house with windows all around, making it bright and airy. During the hot summer months, my cousin Bonnie and I would play under two large arbors and watch the ducks in the pond. How many hours we spent rolling down the slope of Grandma's hill until our clothes and skin would be covered with grass stains!

One of my fondest memories is of Easter at the Big House. Grandma orchestrated not only a traditional Easter egg hunt but also the Great Snail Hunt. She would pass out paper sacks to all her grandchildren, and we would hunt for snails in her flower beds. She paid us a penny for each snail. Grandma was ingenious. We loved it, and she got her flower beds cleaned out once a year!

Laura L. Magnolia Monrovia, CA

Parents Margaret and Charles Little with their daughter Laura; a spectacular view of the Big House.

Suzanne, 6, and Madeline, 9, loved to listen to Grammie Pat tell stories. Pat and sister Dodie (below) played for hours with Lincoln Logs.

IF THE LINCOLN LOG FITS

Sticks of wood spark childhood happiness.

Our imaginations took over when my brother Jim, sister Dolores (aka Dodie) and I brought out the Lincoln Logs. It was the 1940s in Park Ridge, Illinois, and Jim had quite the collection. We built forts, houses, corrals and other farm buildings.

When my granddaughters Suzanne and Madeline visited, I shared stories of my childhood. I also wanted them to have the same fun, so I spent about $300 buying Lincoln Log sets.

When the girls finally outgrew the logs, I advertised them online. A mother and her children came by, and when the kids saw the collection, their eyes lit up. Although I had hoped to recover my money, the look in their eyes melted my heart.

I packed everything into a 13-gallon bag and sold the whole lot for next to nothing. Recalling the joy on their faces still makes me smile. I love knowing someone else is having fun and building memories, too.
Pat Goebel Morris San Diego, CA

DAD'S WORKS OF WONDER

His hand-built Ferris wheels took generations for a ride.

Larry stands by one of his dad's Ferris wheels as he holds the catch of the day (top left). Inspired by his father's miniature Ferris wheels (top right), Larry (right) gives his grandkids Julia (in front) and Ella a whirl on a wheel he built.

Thanks to my dad's building skills and ingenuity, kids flocked to our backyard when I was growing up in the 1960s in Henderson, North Carolina. A 30-foot-tall, four-seat Ferris wheel will do that.

I was about 8 years old when my daddy, James Ellis, built the big red and white wheel. Kids of similar weights sat in opposite seats, then propelled the wheel by pushing off the ground at the bottom of each revolution. Other times, the wheel was Daddy-powered.

It was a very popular attraction. In fact, every spring from third grade on, my class at Clarke Street School would take a short field trip, walking the few blocks to our house just to ride the wheel. Mother and Daddy would serve us popcorn and drinks, and each child would get a ride. Church groups and Boy Scout troops also came to take a spin.

Daddy was no Ferris wheel novice. He built his first one in the 1920s on his own daddy's farm in East Bend. It was a two-seater model, erected between two pine trees. One person would have to climb a tree to get into the top seat.

The tradition continued in the 1980s when we moved to Louisburg, where Daddy built another wheel, this time for my two sons, Jamie and Blair. Their friends, ball teams and other groups came to ride the 30-foot-tall navy blue wheel.

Daddy is gone now, but he inspired me to keep the tradition turning by building my very own four-seater, which now stands in my backyard. My grandchildren love it! At about 20 feet high, it's not nearly as tall as Daddy's Ferris wheels, but I'm sure he'd be proud.

Larry Norman Louisburg, NC

Mom Made a DIY Roller Derby

One couldn't help but smile and laugh at this friendly driveway competition.

The time was around 1951, and the place was Compton, California. Roller Derby was a hot topic around the dinner table. Few families in our neighborhood were lucky enough to have a TV, but those who did would be cheering for the local team, the Los Angeles Thunderbirds. My family had a TV, and we tuned in to Roller Derby weekly.

One sunny day, my mother and Aunt Clara decided they should give Roller Derby a try. Now, mind you, these were two housewives who got dressed up to go to the grocery store and considered planting petunias exercise. They set out picnic benches down the middle of Aunt Clara's driveway to make a rink. The two sisters strapped my cousin Mary Ann's and my skates to their shoes and tied bed pillows to their behinds, then took off around the rink. Granted, they were not going 50 miles per hour, but they tried putting on the steam. This was Roller Derby, for heaven's sake!

It was hilarious. Around and around they went, huffing and puffing for all they were worth, with hair flying, elbows and arms flailing, and I think their tongues were hanging out too. Mary Ann and I—both 8 years old at the time—were cheering wildly for our mothers. The neighbors were hanging over the fence, laughing hysterically.

I don't recall either of them ending up with a cast on anything, and the game was pretty much a draw. But to this day, Mary Ann and I remember that episode and laugh until we are in tears.

Roller Derby was a wonderful way to put excitement and good family entertainment into the lives and homes of friends and neighbors during those times.

Margaret Abel Oliver Reno, NV

One sunny day, my mother and Aunt Clara decided they should give Roller Derby a try.

Doing the real thing, these women from the U.S. roller-skating team are practicing for a Roller Derby bout at Harringay Arena in England.

PACK A PICNIC

Sunshine, good food and fine company.

On Sundays, Dad took us to a beautiful park across town. We'd pack picnic lunches, and many neighbors would come, too. A band would play music on a huge stage.

Linda Quinlivan
Facebook

In Southern California, we would often spend Sunday afternoons in summer at the beach, snacking on chips, cookies and soda while Dad listened to Vin Scully call the Dodger game. When it was time for dinner, he would light up the Coleman camp stove, and Mom would fry thin steaks and saute onions for sandwiches with sides of potato salad and baked beans.

Chris Michalski Hugo
Facebook

We still stop at rest areas to eat, just as I did as a kid. We always have folks come up and share their stories of roadside picnics when they were young, before the interstate highway system. They're glad to see we still do it.

Chris Cochran
Facebook

PICTURE PERFECT

Advances in photography enhanced special family moments.

1950

IN FULL COLOR

Kodacolor film in your camera was "something special," as the results showed off life's true vibrant colors.

1969

GET MORE PHOTOS

Technology improved with the option to have multiple wallet-sized prints of photos — a fantastic way to share photos of little Timmy with the whole family.

Swing Set Sitting

Our daughters Becky, 2, and Debbie, 4, had a ball playing on their sturdy metal swing set. This was taken on a splendid fall afternoon in 1963 in our backyard in Kalamazoo, Michigan.
Sally Grushon Oxford, OH

Tub of Fun

Trying to survive the summer heat was a challenge for our young family in the early 1960s in Scottsdale, Arizona. Daily temperatures often topped 100 degrees. Unable to afford an in-ground pool, we made do with a stainless steel cattle tank. It wasn't the most elegant arrangement, but we certainly enjoyed it!
James G. Lloyd Mesa, AZ

I was apprehensive when my son-in-law climbed the tree to hang that tire swing, but my grandsons Eric Powell and Scott Kelley spent many happy hours on it. This was in 1998 in my backyard.

Patricia Waldron Joppa, MD

Doggie-Roast Tradition

Everyone knew just what to do to make each gathering a success.

Summers in the 1960s stirred up thoughts of long-awaited family picnics that began Memorial Day weekend and continued all summer.

Our family gatherings, known as doggie roasts, took place at my Aunt Ann's in Trenton, New Jersey. She had the perfect backyard, with a towering maple tree that shielded everyone from the hot summer sun. The doggie-roast tradition began in the 1940s and thrived as World War II ended, marriages took place and births of grandchildren were celebrated.

Prepping began two weeks before. Telephone calls between my aunts allowed doggie-roast details to be discussed in depth. You would think my aunts were getting ready for a major political summit rather than a backyard get-together.

Everyone pitched in. Food shopping and ordering rolls from Eagle Bakery were priorities. The day began at 6:30 a.m. Aunt Sophie was in charge of mixing the beef, pork and secret ingredients to make the hamburgers. Karen and I shaped the meat into perfect patties under Aunt Sophie's watchful eye as she inspected each hamburger for size and thickness. "Watch me so you get the next ones right," Aunt Sophie periodically repeated.

The kitchens of my aunts turned out other doggie-roast specialties. Aunt Dot baked casseroles of macaroni and Velveeta cheese. Aunt Gerry fried peppers and onions that topped sizzling hamburgers. My mom made her famous fried sauerkraut that covered plump, juicy hot dogs. Aunt Ann made her famous baked beans.

Uncles Walt and Moe set up tables that consisted of sheets of plywood covered with plastic that were perched on top of wooden sawhorses. Uncle Ed bought bottles of Kern's orange, grape and red cream sodas, which stood like soldiers in a wooden case. Aunts brought lawn chairs for relaxing and old blankets that were transformed into beds for napping young cousins.

The center of attention was the fireplace grill built by Uncle Anthony. Made of stone and fueled by a charcoal briquette fire, it had a sparkling

sheet of stainless steel that served as a cooktop. I recall reruns of *I Love Lucy* and watching the Ricardos and Mertzes build a backyard barbecue. The Ricardo barbecue was a precise replica of the one in Aunt Ann's yard.

The first fry began at 1 p.m. sharp, with Uncle Moe as chief fryer. Hamburgers and hot dogs sizzled on the cooktop. I don't know the secret, but the hamburgers were the best I've ever eaten.

When the first fry and cleanup were completed, pinochle and bingo began. Seated at makeshift card tables, the adults played for hours, taking a break only for a slice of cold, sweet watermelon. When supper time approached, a second fry took place before the final cleanup. Tables were put away, stray bingo chips were plucked from the grass and doggie-roast leftovers were wrapped in waxed paper to take home. Another successful doggie roast was history.

The doggie roasts emphasized the importance of family. I feel blessed for the experience. Food, atmosphere and ritual made it unique. Family bond made it special.

Beverly Sce Yardley, PA

We had lots of picnics and played hundreds of games of cards when I was a kid. Mom and Dad always said they couldn't go to fancy places, so they made their own fun.

Martha H. Williams Burlington, IA

Timeless Delight

My grandfather Wendell Gladstone (foreground) enjoys a picnic with his family in upstate New York in 1936. Among those with him is my Grandmother Ruth, who is holding my mother, Shirley, on her lap.
Wendy Eaton Seattle, WA

Tales of Summertime

Relatives make for lasting childhood memories.

My grandfather loved to tease. It must have been his Irish heritage—although he was born in India. He was the youngest son of an Irish father who was serving in Her Majesty's 39th Regiment as a sergeant in India. Grandfather would speak Hindi, which we didn't understand, of course, but we would "interpret" into wild tales.

I must say, though, the most fun came from my mom's siblings, my Aunt Mary and my Uncle Ron. Aunt Mary lived a rural life on British Columbia's Cortes Island, where we enjoyed many summer holidays. Uncle Ron, the youngest of the clan, hosted family reunions at his home in Penticton. Both had lots of zany ideas to keep us kids busy. As we got older, the activities aged along with us and always included the adults as well.

On Cortes, we would enjoy evenings of stoop tag or a game of baseball on the cowpie-filled field, which necessitated some pretty fancy footwork. While sleeping in the hayloft, we'd listen to the night sounds and let our imaginations run away with us.

There were Saturday night dances, for which a logging truck would pick us up and transport us across the island. As only three people could fit in the cab of the truck, heavy timbers, running the length of the truck bed, were secured to the bunkers that normally carried logs. We'd all sit back to back on each side of these "timber seats." Placement was exact to make sure children had a seat between two adults who could hold on to them. Once we were underway, the singalong would start as we traveled the narrow road.

In Penticton at the family reunions, we'd enjoy lakeside activities at Skaha or Okanagan Lake, depending which way the wind blew. Wiener roasts were held around the backyard fire pit, which allowed lots of time for reminiscing. The family reunions always wound up with a huge spaghetti feed—Uncle Ron's specialty.

Several years after our last family reunion, my husband and I traveled from Alberta and took our children camping along the Similkameen River. We invited Uncle Ron and family to join us. He suggested that he prepare a big spaghetti supper for us that could be reheated over our open campfire. We agreed, and when everyone was ready to eat, Uncle Ron said he had to check the sauce one last time. As he bent over the fire, he popped his false teeth into his hand to better taste the sauce. Our kids had never seen such a thing and sat bug-eyed until we all started laughing. That was a typical Uncle Ron joke.

We're often told that laughter is the best medicine. I sure have a large store of happy moments to draw on.

Elaine Durst Kelowna, BC

Picnic at Sandy Beach on Cortes; Penticton family reunion, 1963.

Playtime Pipes

New culvert pipes awaited installation in my Beaumont, Texas, neighborhood in 1960. Meanwhile, my daughter Susie climbed aboard as her cousins, (from left) Charlie, Glen and John Snell, crawled inside. That's my 1955 Studebaker Champion parked at the curb. I wish I still had that car.

Bill Sweikert DeRidder, LA

Park Outing

Here I am on an afternoon outing with my three kids in 1965. I'm holding baby John while daughter Michele gives my leg a bear hug. Kathleen looks as though she's seriously contemplating a swim in the water at Riverside Park in Riverside, California. My wife, Lillian, took the photo on this perfect summer day.

Donald Malone Leesburg, TX

Flight Plan

One bright autumn day in the 1970s, I took advantage of the weather to fly model airplanes at a nearby park with my sons Bruce and Billy.
Odette Landers Fort Pierce, FL

Loving Parents

My mother, Rosalie Thompson, and I have fun at a small lake in California in 1947. This image brings back memories of my mother's love and also of my talented father, Alec, who not only took the picture but developed and printed it in a darkroom that he built.
Darlene Van Hemelryck Page, AZ

Not Just for the Birds

Back in 1968, the Norton clan took over the Noonan Park "duck house,"
a kids' favorite at this Minnesota lake where waterfowl migrate each year.
Jim Norton Alexandria, MN

Flying High

My mother, Rose, and I smile for the camera on the umbrella ride at Idora Park in Youngstown, Ohio, in 1968. My father, Frank, the photographer, was riding in the seat just behind us with one of my siblings. Spending a day at one of the many amusement parks nearby was a perfect mini vacation for our big family.
Susan Dietrich Monaca, PA

Snowfall Sparked Imaginations

Getting into the proper gear was part of the fun.

During the winter of 1966-'67, my three brothers—Jerry, Joe and Jeff—and I couldn't wait to get outside to play. I was the oldest; baby Kathy had just arrived. (I guess Mom and Dad had run out of names beginning with J.)

We lived in Stoutsville, Ohio, a town of 500 about 30 miles south of Columbus. Stoutsville had no stoplight, and downtown the railroad tracks crossed Main Street next to a restaurant.

Our house was a humble two-story, three-bedroom abode. We boys slept on bunk beds, Army-barracks style, in one bedroom.

The house was heated by an oil furnace in the basement that sounded like a plane taking off under the kitchen when it kicked on.

Getting dressed was a production. We didn't have fancy-schmancy down-filled snowsuits or Gore-Tex ski pants. Instead, we started with white flannel long underwear and layered on hand-me-down jeans and shirts from our older cousins. We topped it all off with hand-me-down hooded winter jackets.

From our house, we trooped across a gravel lane to a huge yard. In spring, we flew kites there on a carpet of grass. Now it was covered with snow, and we built snowmen, forts, angels, igloos—the possibilities were endless.

After hours outside, we were hungry, tired, wet and cold. We tromped back across the lane and hung our clothes in the basement. Mom fixed us hot chocolate, and we waited to hear the airplane in the basement take off. Then we scrambled to sit on the heat registers in the floor. Ah, bliss.

John Scanlan Hilton Head Island, SC

Joe and Jeff (who looks ready to go inside) stand in the foreground with Jerry and John behind.

Rosy Cheeks

My children Bruce and Debbie could hardly wait to take their new sled out on a snowy January morning in 1968. The snow was packed just right in the lane, and they had so much fun!
Mary Brown Flat Rock, IL

One Sled, Two Smiles

After a fresh snowfall while visiting Grandma and Grandpa in Gilbertsville, Pennsylvania, in 1976, my kids, Sherri and Jeff, enjoyed the beautiful winter wonderland (below).
Karin Rasmussen Grass Valley, CA

What a Ride

My son Rusty took his little brother Travis (above) for a walk to see their grandmother. Nanny burst out laughing when she opened the door.
Zelda Rowley Lancaster, PA

Stylish Skiers
Here is my dad with my brother Jim at Diamond Hill Park in Cumberland in 1959. From the looks on their faces, I can't help but wonder if they were reconsidering tackling the intermediate hill.
Christine Tremblay
Cumberland, Rhode Island

Stacked Up
Silly snow play was the theme of the afternoon when this photo of my youngest sisters was taken in our front yard in Kankakee, Illinois, in 1948. Linda piled on top of the twins, Rosemary and Barbara.
Jackie Cross Bonfield, IL

939   FrAN   JAY   Eddie   ossie   DAd

It took six of us—my sisters (Fran and Jay),
my husband (Eddie), my brother-in-law (Ossie), Dad
and me—to roll this monster-sized snowball back
in 1939. You needed a lot of open space to roll a
snowball this size! It measured 5 feet in diameter.
Ann Simonini Darien, IL

NHL Bound?
In 1961, my brothers and
I were eager to use the
skates we'd received for
Christmas, so Dad (Ken)
made us a rink in our
backyard in Marengo,
Wisconsin. With me
(second from left) are Lynn,
Kevin, Dad, Lee and Roger.
Kathleen J. Coleman Morton, WA

Colossal Snowman

My twin granddaughters, Lyndsay and Meggan Burud, age 11, pose with a giant snow creation in Hermantown, Minnesota, near our home in Duluth.
James H. Burud Duluth, MN

Winter Safari

Jean, Don and Greg Pippin enjoy a cold Massachusetts day in 1964. Oh, wait—we're ignoring the elephant in the room! Our family built this six-foot-long pachyderm over two days, and we even got our picture in the local paper.
Pippin family

Flakey Friends
My sons Bruce, 5, and Mark, 4, made some new friends in our backyard in Blaine, Minnesota, in 1966.
Annette Borup Hanson
Grantsburg, WI

Larger than Life
My daughter Cathy, 4, stands next to a 9-foot snowman in front of our Bound Brook, New Jersey, home in December 1964.
Steve Chubrick Largo, FL

Bob Sprankle's improvised iceboat was one more way to get the family outdoors in the Pennsylvania winter.

Coming in Hot!

Dad's invention was ice fun. Until it wasn't.

Our family had so much fun skating on the river that Dad decided to give the old airboat a winter makeover. Down in his workshop, our dad, Bob Sprankle, sawed, pounded and painted. He fired and bent steel bologna hooks into skate runners for the boat. Our mom, Marian, sewed a canvas sail that was so heavy it took several of my uncles and cousins to hoist it up the mast.

One icy January day in 1960, we hauled the iceboat to Glendale Lake. The ice was deep green, buffed smooth by the wind. Dad and Uncle Ab pushed the contraption onto the lake, and Mom was in charge of the new 8 mm movie camera.

Uncle Ab steered the skate at the front, while Dad worked the two on the sides and manned the sail. My younger sister Pammie, 5, and I clung to the outriggers.

A breeze kissed the sail and it bellowed. The boat eased forward and the relatives watching cheered. Oh, my goodness, was it fun! The wind picked up. We skimmed faster and faster across the ice. Dad was thrilled—one of his creations finally worked. The crowd ran along the shore, waving and shouting. We laughed and waved back.

Now we were going so fast my eyes stung and my cheeks burned. I glanced at Dad and his face was beet red. Uncle Ab shouted, "Stop this thing—we're headed for the dam!"

"Turn the skate!" Dad yelled.

"I can't. It's stuck. Pull the brake!" Uncle Ab shouted.

"There is no brake!" Dad's voice was shrill. "I forgot to build one!"

Pammie and I clung to our perches; if we let go now, we'd surely be angels.

"The dam, the dam!" Uncle Ab screamed. "Drop the sail!"

"It's knotted," Dad yelled.

Uncle Ab ferreted in his pocket for a knife. Out flew his keys, cigarettes and lighter. Finally, he tossed the knife to Dad, who sawed the rope, bringing the sail crashing down the mast. The boat slid to a stop inches from the dam.

My mom caught it all on camera, so now and then we set up the projector and watch the movie. Cheering as the iceboat glides, gasping as it soars, and sighing relief as it stops just short of disaster.

Susie Sprankle Walls Tyrone, PA

LITTLE BUNDLE

I love how my mom and dad, Doris and Jim Carroll, used this old box to make
a sleigh seat for my brother Eddie, 16 months, in Rosedale, New York, in 1947.

Doris Maiorino North Babylon, NY

MAKE 'EM LAUGH

Goofing around is definitely a part of family life. These photos and tales of just being silly together are bound to make you smile.

A VERY WARM MEMORY

Dad got a bit hot under the collar about this assignment.

My mother, Jo, volunteered to play Smokey Bear for the Arbor Day festival at our Cocoa Beach nursery school in 1965. But when she got the costume, she realized it was far too big for her.

No problem, she thought, *Lane is tall; he can wear it*. Dad wasn't happy about being volunteered, but he put on the costume anyway.

The day was very warm, with the Florida sunshine bright and hot. The costume was made of thick fur, and Dad started sweating profusely. To make matters worse, the bear head was too large for Dad to sit upright in our station wagon; he had to lie down in the bed behind the backseat with his head poking out the rear window.

On our ride to school, people were honking, waving and slamming on their brakes to get a better look at the bear in our car. At school, a teacher had to guide Dad around because he couldn't see out of the eyes.

My little sister, Debbie, was so afraid of the giant bear that Dad had to take the head off to prove it was really him.

Despite his discomfort, Dad helped to make the festival a success. Many pine seedlings were planted that day.

Back home, he swore he'd sweated away 10 pounds. That was the first and last time Mom volunteered our father for anything.

Becky McGregor Orlando, FL

Becky, Debbie and Guy stand with their dad, Lane Arbuthnot, dressed as Smokey, at their school's Arbor Day festival in 1965.

Rude Awakening

Sunday sermon sent her husband into hysterics.

As we parked our motor home at a North Carolina campsite on a lovely Saturday afternoon in the late 1970s, my husband noticed a loudspeaker on a tree right above us. When Wayne asked the campground manager about it, he assured us it wasn't turned on.

Relieved by his answer, we drove down to the ocean, where our children unloaded beach gear from a storage pod atop our vehicle. I retrieved our portable radio, but it wouldn't work. I jiggled and shook it and turned the dials—nothing. I figured the batteries must be dead. We enjoyed the sun and sand without it, then drove back to the campground and went to bed early.

The next morning, the shouting of an overzealous evangelist jolted us out of a sound sleep. "Praise Jesus!" the voice said. "Join me now, sinners. Get down on your knees and pray for forgiveness!"

Wayne jumped out of bed, yelling as loudly as the preacher. He didn't even bother to don

flip-flops or a robe; he just ran to the manager's office and pounded on the door. The manager dutifully followed him back to our site and looked up at the speaker. Wayne kept yelling, even as the manager assured him the campground's sound system was turned off.

By now, a few early morning travelers had gathered. His patience wearing thin, Wayne climbed the ladder on our motor home to remove the speaker, until he realized the sound wasn't coming from the speaker but from our storage pod. He opened it and found our radio—the one I'd assumed wasn't working—blaring the preacher's sermon!

Wayne slowly descended the ladder, his face turning several shades of red. As the crowd dispersed and the manager walked away, shaking his head, we slunk inside our vehicle and quickly got dressed. Then we headed to Florida a week earlier than planned.

Jane Lindstedt Hermitage, PA

Teaching Tom the Turkey a Lesson

Luckily, Grandpa would never have to know about it.

Tom was Grandpa Hein's old male turkey. He was just plain mean—an aggressive, strutting bully. Since my family lived on his western Iowa farm during the Depression era, Grandpa was allowed to have a mean turkey if he wanted. So Tom dominated everything weaker than himself, like chickens, cats and us kids. Before stepping through the gate and into the barnyard, we kids would carefully look around. Tom would attack by pecking us with his beak or raking us with his sharp toenails and long leg spurs. To me, a seven-year-old boy, Tom the turkey looked fierce with his bald head, red-white-and-blue waddle, dangling snood and evil beady eyes. But he knew his limitations and never attacked adults, so Grandpa, a tough old German "turkey" himself, liked Tom.

One cold fall day, Dad was splitting our winter wood in the barnyard. I was helping, kid fashion, by getting in the way. Then there came terrible Tom, the terror turkey. Dad noticed that I'd circled around to place him between Tom and me. Like most hard-times farmers, Dad was a tough guy and thought his young son should be too. He picked up a slender pole lying on the woodpile, handed it to me, and instructed me to step out and defend myself.

Tom strutted closer and closer, back and forth, his evil eye on me. When he got within pole range, with Dad's backup and coaching, I swung the pole as hard as I could. More by luck than by good aim, I cracked Tom on the back of his bald head. He flopped down on his side, clawed at his head a couple of times and lay still. Dad and I just stared, both stunned by the sudden turn of events. Then Dad picked up Tom's listless body and carried it to the back corner of our machine shed. "Don't tell Grandpa, and let's see what happens," he told me.

The next day, Tom was out and about with a big blue lump on his naked head. After that, he would still chase cats and chickens but never me! Whenever I approached, he would turkey trot in the opposite direction. My early life lesson was that bullies are really cowards if you call their bluff. Of course, it helps to have your dad, a big former football player, standing right behind you.

Richard N. Rife The Dalles, OR

"YES, CHICKENS EAT GRAVEL!"

Dad was a joker, so his suggestions were sometimes met with hesitation.

My father taught me the meaning of having someone "pull your leg." Dad told me that the way to catch a bird was to sneak up on it and put salt on its tail. So my cousins and I spent hours trying to catch blue jays and chickadees, to no avail. Much later, I realized there was no magic in this trick: If you were close enough to a bird to salt it, you were close enough to grab it!

My dad also advised us kids about fishing: "If it's winter and you're going ice fishing," he said, "always hold the worms in your mouth for a few minutes to warm them up. Fish don't like cold food." I can't imagine how Mom would have reacted if we had done this!

So I was skeptical when he asked me to get a pan of gravel for the chickens to eat. Huh? I had seen chickens eat corn and grain, but I had never seen them eat gravel! Still, my mom was holding out an old metal pie plate, so I went to the edge of our dirt road, filled the pan with gravel and put it in the coop.

To my surprise, the chickens were absolutely thrilled! They hopped and pushed one another out of the way, unable to get enough of the gravel bits for themselves. My dad explained this as it had been explained to him as a child: "Chickens don't have stomachs full of digestive juices like we do. They have gullets. They need gravel to rub against the corn or grain to break it down and get nutrition from the food."

Cheryl Lawrence Springfield, VT

I had seen chickens eat corn and grain, but I had never seen them eat gravel!

These two feed a flock of chickens that seem to be just as thrilled of the spoils as the chickens Cheryl fed.

MOM FLIPPED HER WIG OVER FAMILY PHOTO

Help came just in the nick of time.

My mom decided to get a family portrait taken for our church directory in the 1970s. When the big day came, all six of us children—ages 7 to 21—miraculously managed to get home on time and make the short drive to St. Francis of Assisi Church, located in Athol Springs, New York.

Then I noticed that poor Mom, who'd made sure everyone was fed and had something clean and ironed to wear, didn't have time to curl her own hair. So I gave her my new auburn Kanekalon wig, fashionably cut and styled.

When it was our turn to get photographed, I saw that Mom, who'd never worn a wig before, had it on backward! I quickly walked over and nonchalantly flipped the face-framing curly side to the front before we took our seats.

No one else in the room noticed, except for Dad and us kids (that's me, standing on the right). We couldn't help but snicker. The smiles in this picture are for real! As you can see, Mom looks very happy to finally get a family photo taken—even though we all had trouble staying composed.

My parents still prominently display this photo in their living room, and most of their 13 grandchildren know the story about the day Grandma literally flipped her wig.

Linda Hammer Demler Jamestown, NY

Grandma Knew Best

But the teacher didn't see it that way.

When I was a junior in high school in Scotland County, North Carolina, in 1949, our home economics teacher assigned a project to make a skirt with an invisible zipper. She showed us how it was done, and I went home excited to begin my new skirt.

After making the skirt, I proceeded to struggle with the invisible zipper, not knowing that my grandmother was watching. She finally came over and told me that I was doing it wrong. My grandmother happened to be a great seamstress, so I let her show me how it was done.

The next day in school, I was called on to demonstrate how to put in an invisible zipper. As I was doing this, my teacher stopped me, saying that was not the way she had taught me. I told her my grandmother had shown me an easier way. The teacher became angry and sent me to the principal's office. And that is how I got kicked out of home economics class.

I had the last laugh, though, because I became a gifted seamstress myself and even taught friends how to sew and put in their own invisible zippers.

Alise Guinn Tega Cay, SC

Alise stands with her grandmother Bertha Ethel Blakeley, who shared tips and tricks for easier sewing.

Donning Hats

My grandfather Joseph Urtz (top center) and five of his sons posed for this picture in Ilion, New York, in 1944, when everybody wore hats. My father, Clarence, is on the bottom left. Also pictured are Jerome (top left), Joe (top right), Paul (bottom center) and Robert. I love this picture. Anybody who sees it says it looks like something out of *The Godfather*.
Donald Urtz Richfield Springs, NY

The Battle of the Bike

He took drastic action to commandeer the Big Trike.

(Top) Jerry savors a moment on the Big Trike with sisters Elizabeth (left) and Ruth. He drove a smaller set of wheels (above) before riding the prized Big Trike.

The Big Trike was one sweet ride. I remember when it arrived at our house in Milwaukee in the 1950s: blue with white pinstripes, a red seat and a front wheel twice the size of a normal tricycle wheel. It rode like the wind; no one in our entire neighborhood could beat it in a race.

My tomboy sister, Elizabeth, who was 18 months older and beat me at everything, thought the Big Trike was hers because it arrived around her seventh birthday. But I knew the trike was meant to be shared. That spelled trouble, because she and I defined sibling rivalry. In fact, whenever Ma wasn't around, I called her Lazy Lizzie Lizard.

One day I decided it was my turn to ride the Big Trike. But no matter how hard I tried, I couldn't pry the Lizard's hands off the handlebars.

So I implemented Plan B. I figured if I blocked the sidewalk, the Lizard would have to stop and go get Ma. (We didn't dare ride on Pa's lawn.) Then I'd hop on the Big Trike and ride until dinner—that is, if I even got any. It seemed worth the risk.

So I lay down on my back, across the sidewalk. About 30 seconds later, the Lizard came blasting into view. It almost seemed as though she picked up speed when she saw the human speed bump ahead, but I wasn't worried; I knew the Big Trike could stop on a dime.

Then, *whump*! The front wheel ran over my stomach. Now stopped in her tracks, the Lizard ran inside the house to get Ma, just as I'd figured she would. I, however, found myself stuck, wedged between the front and rear wheels.

When Ma came outside to free me, guess who got punished. But I didn't want supper anyway—I had a tummy ache.

Jerry Wessel McKees Rocks, PA

Ill-Fit Cowboys

Taken in Brockton, Massachusetts, in 1937, this photo shows me, 4, standing beside my 10-year-old brother. Both of us are clearly dressed to impress. Our uncle sent us two cowboy outfits complete with hats and neckerchiefs. The outfits were the same size, so mine was way too big and my brother's was way too small.

George Brouillette Groton, MA

Curly Connection

There were no tests back then, so after I was born on May 19, 1931, my sister Christine surprised my mom. We were the talk of our small town of Westby, Wisconsin. I was short with black hair and dark eyes. Christine was tall, blond and blue-eyed.

Catherine Schlicht Viroqua, WI

Good Old-Fashioned Fun

Times have changed, but a young boy's amusements are still amusing.

Sporadic radio programs were about the only entertainment we had in 1928. My dad was a storyteller par excellence, so we four boys would gather in a semicircle to listen to him, sitting cross-legged by his knees.

My dad, the first of three boys and three girls, was born in 1881 in Hoboken, New Jersey, near the Hudson River. There was never much money, but the family had a good life. He learned not to mention the few pennies he might earn from a stranger for running an errand. His mother would confiscate the money to add to a jar for the family's use.

Kids could run their neighborhoods without fear in those days, and Dad and his brother Sam took full advantage of that freedom. Close by were swamps teeming with muskrats to trap and sloughs with fish to catch or ducks to hunt. Now these places are buried in huge piles of garbage.

When life became a bit boring, they played a game: They slipped up behind a lady and gently placed a pebble on the bustle beneath her long dress, watching it bounce along until it fell. Two bustled women walking together would each be adorned with a pebble at the same moment, and bets were exchanged on whose pebble would bounce the longest.

There were horse-drawn vehicles everywhere. Drivers of small freight wagons had bullwhips to pep up their horses, and they delighted, on occasion, in cutting a buttonhole on the rump of an unwary boy of seven or eight years. Both my dad and his brother were recipients of this painful whip snap. Derisive laughter would follow their hopping about as they held their rears. Revenge was in the air.

The boys made slingshots; I don't know how they were constructed, but they were powerful. The brothers hid, waited until the wagon driver had passed, and then stepped out from cover and peppered the back of their antagonist with small stones or a palmful of buckshot. The brothers were delighted if their shots raised puffs of dust from the whipper's back.

There were many places where kids could slip off to swim. Big lads taught the younger ones by tossing them into the pool and letting them dog paddle their way to shore. The youngsters learned quickly, and no boy was allowed to drown. They never told their parents where these swimming holes were, because then the folks would know where to look for them on a hot summer day when there were chores to do.

One sweltering day, my dad and Uncle Sam slipped off to their favorite swimming hole for a cool dip. They went in buck naked, as swimsuits were too spendy for the family's money jar. The swimming area was in a very slow-moving stream, and before they realized it, they had drifted a considerable distance. The low sun told them it was time to get home. They swam back to their entry spot and climbed up the bank to the old oak tree where they had left their clothes. They were gone! Every last stitch of them—gone. Shoes, shirts, knee pants, socks—gone. They ran home barefoot, wrapped in old newspapers and in shame, and accompanied by ribald laughter.

Barry Naugle Emmett, ID

Kids splash about in a swimming hole much like the one Barry's father visited in his youth.

Little Miss Unpopular

Mom's pageant coaching got her booed off the stage.

During election season, my thoughts always go back to 1936, when my mother entered me in a beauty contest at a local movie theater in Guthrie, Oklahoma. I was 4 years old at the time and had curly blond hair, so Mom often dressed me like Shirley Temple. For the competition that evening, I wore a frilly blue dress with black patent leather shoes, blue socks and a matching blue headband.

On the day of the beauty contest, Mom and I entered the theater through the stage door, and I found myself in a forest of legs! All the other contestants were young ladies wearing swimsuits.

The contest organizers led us onto the stage, where they pointed out an X marked on the floor. They told us to walk to the X, pose and preen, turn around so the judges could look us over and then leave the stage the way we had entered.

When it was my time to shine, I strutted out there, and the crowd started oohing and aahing. I was definitely something different. I posed, twirled around and then did what my mother, an avid political campaigner, had coached me to do. I raised my hand and shouted, "Vote for Alf Landon!"

What had been an adoring audience became a booing crowd. They scared the daylights out of me! I forgot all about going back the way I'd come in, ran the opposite way—straight into a brick wall—and knocked myself out.

Gov. Landon of Kansas was running against the beloved incumbent, Franklin D. Roosevelt, for president that year. I lost the competition, and Alf Landon lost the election.

Lucina Bradford White Monroe, MI

Say "Cheese"!
On Sept. 8, 1993, their first day back at school, Matthew, 9, and Sarah, 8, look prepared. Less-than-excited little brother Brian, 7, could use a nap.
Mike McCrobie Oswego, NY

Worth the Wait
Meeting Bozo the Clown and his co-stars thrilled my daughters Kristi and Karen in May 1969. After applying for tickets, we had to wait three years before we got our turn to attend the show at Chicago's WGN-TV studios! Our fan club—including (front row) Kristi, two neighborhood pals and Karen—clowned around backstage with (back row) Oliver O. Oliver, Bozo, Ringmaster Ned and Sandy.
David Burnett Naples, FL

Coming to Grips with a Sticky Situation

The lollipop seemed like the perfect solution, until it wasn't.

Perhaps I shouldn't have taken my toddler to the grocery store at naptime. Kelly was reaching for everything and trying to climb out of the child seat. In desperation, I reached into the "emergency" section of my purse and pulled out an orange lollipop. Kelly's face lit up as I unwrapped the treat and handed it to her.

Now I'll be able to concentrate, I thought. I browsed through my coupons, thankful that Kelly was busy and content.

I was so engrossed in finding good deals that I didn't notice the sugary drool dripping down Kelly's chin. It wasn't until she placed a wet, sticky hand on my blouse that I took a good look at her. The mess was stunning. Almost every inch of her face was sticky. Her shirt was sticky. She was sticky from her fingertips to her elbows. She grinned at me, then stuck out her orange tongue.

Since I was holding at least 40 coupons in my left hand, I dug through my pockets with my right, looking for a tissue. I pulled out a small napkin and tried wiping her face. It gave her a paper beard. As I tried to peel it off, she grabbed at the stack of coupons in my other hand and flung them upward. The top and bottom coupon in the stack stuck tight to her hand, but every one in between was launched into orbit.

For a moment, it was a captivating sight. Coupons of every size rained down in a silent flutter. But as soon as they came in contact with my child, they glued fast. Her blue eyes peered over the margarine coupon affixed to her nose. She tried to pull it off, but the paper towel coupon on her hand was in the way. The coupons on each little cheek flapped as she called out, "Mama!"

Her alarmed voice seemed to be the only sound in the store. All eyes were on us. The other shoppers froze in awe, until a few of them started to giggle. Coupons were on the shopping cart handle, and some were littered around my shoes.

I had to buy baby wipes to clean her up. The worst part was that I just knew I had a coupon for them…somewhere.

Marianne Fosnow Fort Mill, SC

Kelly's face lit up as I unwrapped the treat and handed it to her.

Lollipops like these can be quite troublesome in the hands of a toddler.

(Above) Rose Mary, Robert, Charles, Elbert Jr., Walter and Don pose with their mother (third from right) on Mother's Day 1964. (Right) Witten clan in 1974: Charles, Walter, Elbert Jr., Robert, Rose Mary and Don. (Below) Mary Witten in 1926, the year she married.

Prayers Answered

Family lore has it that my mother, Mary, had been praying for a girl, but when her sixth child was born, she mistook the umbilical cord for something else. "Oh my God," she cried. "Another boy." The nurse, Sister Rose Xavier, came to the rescue. "No, Mary, it's a girl. See!" So Mary called her only daughter Rose Mary in the nurse's honor.
Don Witten Columbia, MD

WHAT MOM SAID

I like to believe mothers can teach the big things in life with these small popular sayings. I used some of them on my children and grandchildren. Hey, if it works, it works.

Janice Jones Kingsport, TN

RELIGION
"You better pray that will come out of the carpet."

LOGIC
"If you fall and break your neck, you won't be able to come to the store with me."

GENEALOGY
"Stop acting like your father."

OSMOSIS
"Shut your mouth and eat your supper."

STAMINA
"You'll sit there until your spinach is gone."

METEOROLOGY
"Your room looks as if a tornado went through it."

PLANNING FOR THE FUTURE, PART I
"Make sure you wear clean underwear in case you're in an accident."

PLANNING FOR THE FUTURE, PART II
"When you get to be my age, you'll understand."

Always Time for a Laugh
My dad, Lawrence Arnold, goofs around with my sister Williamette in our Lebanon, Pennsylvania, backyard in 1938. We were a pretty fun family, even back then.
Rosemarie Hess Lebanon, PA

THEN

Pictured from left to right are John Brubaker, Edward Brubaker, Evelyn Glasscock, Robert Brubaker, Marie Kemp, Richard Brubaker, Warren Brubaker and Charles.

NOW

My husband, Charles Brubaker, and his seven siblings took both of these photos on their front porch in Luray, Virginia—one in 1947, the other in 2012. Bravo to the Brubaker clan—every adult adopted the same expression from the childhood photo, and Richard even sat in his sister Marie's lap!

Gail Brubaker Luray, VA

CUTE AS A BUTTON?

These curly haired babies just might get you to buy these products.

1948

LITTLE PEANUT

The naked Karo Kid began appearing in the 1940s. A picture of innocence, the boy was meant to convey the purity of Karo syrup.

1947

ROLE REVERSAL

The giant baby in this Johnson & Johnson ad is schooling his baby-sized mother in infant skin care.

Save the Cake!

This baker will never forget her family's birthday blowout.

A couple of years ago I made quite the kitchen blunder getting things just right for a special celebration. I usually don't cause many mishaps, but I committed one that certainly took the cake in this particular instance.

For a family birthday party in January, I put together a beautiful two-layered white confection topped with chocolate whipped cream frosting—my daughter Alicia's favorite. It was something to behold, but not for long!

Before serving the dessert, I placed the cake on our glass-top stove. I hadn't yet heated up the homemade chocolate syrup for our ice cream, so I put the small pan in a bigger pan of water on a back burner and turned the heat up high. Then I began preparing a plate of cookies.

All of a sudden I heard a loud pop! Alicia turned to find the source of the strange noise, soon discovering that I had accidentally turned on the front burner holding the glass cake plate.

The heat was too much for the refrigerated plate, which had cracked beneath the cake.

I ran over to the stove and turned off the burner, horrified by what I saw. Glass pieces from the shattered plate were shooting out in all directions, and the stove was scorching bits of cake that had fallen into the burner, sending smoke throughout the entire house. Everyone was opening up windows and doors to let the smoke out.

Alicia screamed, "Save the cake! Save the cake!" I had my hands full trying to rescue the birthday treat. At last I miraculously removed it from the burner using two pancake turners.

Scared to serve the whole cake, I cut only the top layer. Before we began eating, I warned anyone who bit on something crunchy to tell the rest of us. Fortunately, no one found anything, and we all enjoyed what was left of my delicious creation.

Marlagene Andersen Perry, IA

ALL SMILES

My Aunt Mabel let loose with her mom, Carrie, on a spring day around 1956.
Mabel (right) looked like a tough woman, but she had a fantastic sense of humor.

Thomas W. Metz Allentown, PA

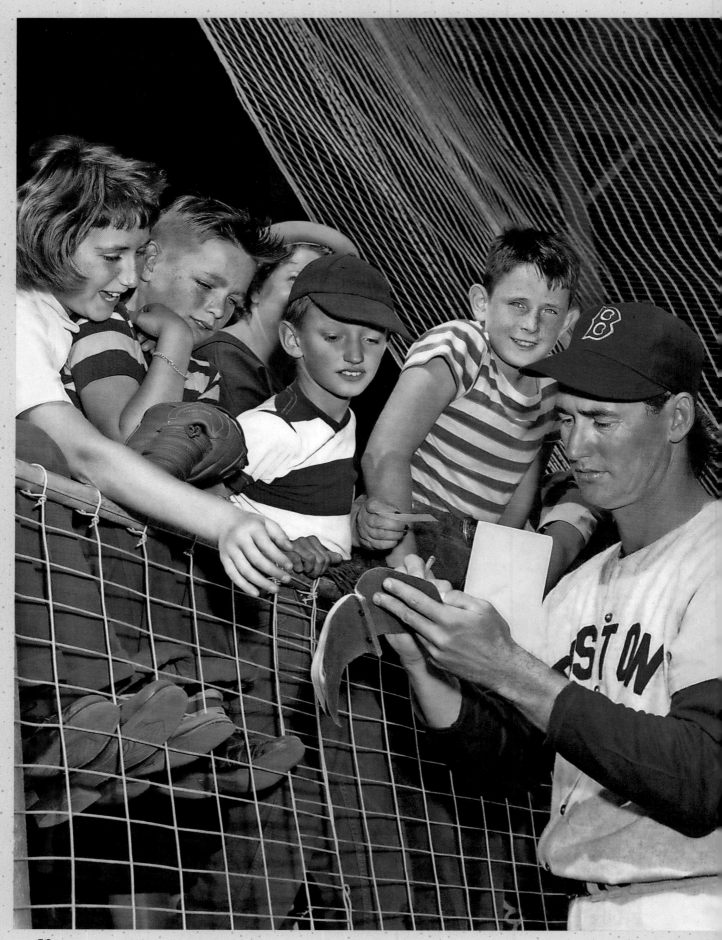

THAT'S ENTERTAINMENT

Enjoying a movie, a concert, the circus or a ballgame with loved ones was as exciting back in the day as it is now.

The Night Debbie Reynolds Was Dad's Girlfriend

Dinner show proves to be a lasting family memory.

O n a family trip to Lake Tahoe in 1975, my dad tried to get tickets to see Sammy Davis Jr., but that event was sold out. He came back with tickets for the Debbie Reynolds dinner show instead. I wasn't expecting much, to be honest. Debbie definitely did not have Sammy's hip-cool factor.

My dad, always outgoing and gregarious, was dressed in his bright yellow slacks and jacket with white patent leather shoes. He was sporting his signature goatee, too. He tipped the maitre d' and we got a front-row table.

No sooner had the show started than Debbie sashayed off the stage, into the audience and straight up to my father, Wayne. She sat flirtatiously in his lap and talked to him while stroking his goatee. After learning my mother's name, Evadale, Debbie had the entire audience shout, "Hi, Wayne! How's Little Eva?" That became the catchphrase of the evening.

She continued to mention my father at various points throughout her show. For example, when a cast member who was a bodybuilder flexed his muscles, Debbie quipped, "Wayne taught him how to do that." Then she'd signal for the catchphrase and the audience would shout, "Hi, Wayne! How's Little Eva?"

Debbie's show was fantastic that night with its singing, dancing, chorus line, gorgeous costumes and humor. Best of all, she gave my father a taste of the limelight, a place he loved to be.

After the show, numerous people in the casino greeted Dad with the catchphrase—even hours later as we were walking into a different casino.

I'm sure Sammy Davis Jr.'s performance was great, but I can't imagine he would have perched on Dad's lap and made him a part of his act.

The Gurneys—Lou Ann, Evadale and Wayne—relax in their Lake Tahoe hotel room before going to Debbie Reynolds' dinner show in 1975. Note that Wayne wears his snazzy white patent shoes.

Debbie Reynolds created a treasured memory for us.

Forever after, we referred to Debbie Reynolds as "Dad's girlfriend."

Lou Ann Gurney Keaau, HI

SURPRISE ROLE CALL

People saw double when his dad worked with Cary Grant.

Cary Grant double Augustine DeCesare, aka Danny Cassell, strides through a movie set in 1946.

My father, Augustine DeCesare, had one of the most unusual jobs in the world: a stand-in for legendary actor Cary Grant.

Dad was born in New Haven, Connecticut, and never planned on becoming an actor. But when he went to California around 1942, he got a job as a movie extra, using the stage name Danny Cassell. One day a casting agent spotted him. In a matter of hours, my father was shaking hands with Archibald Alexander Leach—which is how Cary Grant introduced himself, using his real name.

This twist of fate amazed Dad. As he said in a newspaper article in the 1940s, "I had no illusions about Hollywood… and I was just as surprised as anyone could be when I was told I was to be a stand-in for Cary."

Dad worked in about a half-dozen movies with Grant, including *Notorious*, *The Bachelor and the Bobby-Soxer*, *The Bishop's Wife* and *Mr. Blandings Builds His Dream House*. He earned $50 per movie, plus free lunches on the set. Another perk: He met a lot of movie stars, including Victor Mature, Danny Kaye, Loretta Young, Shirley Temple, Eddie Albert, David Niven and Ingrid Bergman.

As for Grant, Dad really liked him. He said that Grant was an unassuming guy, a regular Joe—a rarity for a Hollywood star. In fact, he told me he even double-dated with the actor.

In the late '40s, Grant began spending more time away from Hollywood and Dad eventually moved back to Connecticut. There he met and married my mom, Gloria, and worked for a company that made refrigerator units for rockets and aircraft. My father, who passed away in 2010 at age 97, always talked proudly about his brief career in Hollywood.

Ken DeCesare Mountain View, CA

An Afternoon with the Duke

At 13, kindness leaves a lasting impression.

One cold morning in March 1955, my parents decided to take a road trip from our rural farm in Tacoma, Washington, to Southern California. We went to visit my dad's family—my grandfather, uncles, aunts and cousins. My mom and dad left the farm in the hands of the neighbors and, along with my brother, 5, and my grandma, we all piled into the car and headed south on Old 99.

I don't remember how many days we traveled, but I remember being annoyed by my younger brother even before we hit the Oregon border. There was constant seat switching so we could both survive the miles. I was upset because I knew Disneyland wasn't opening until July, and I couldn't understand why my parents wouldn't wait to take this trip.

Once we got to California, we spent a day at Knott's Berry Farm and Olvera Street (the historic market). Then one day my Uncle Don, a freelance photographer for the movie studios, invited me to spend a day at work with him. My parents agreed.

So they took me to the Hollywood Robert Hall store, where I got a new outfit, and the next morning Uncle Don picked me up. I was nervous but excited, especially when he said I was going to meet a couple of movie stars.

When we got to the studio, a scene was being shot, and everything was quiet. How thrilling! At lunch, Uncle Don took me to meet the stars—Lauren Bacall and John Wayne. They were shooting a scene for the movie *Blood Alley*.

Lauren Bacall sat for a photo and then walked away. But John Wayne was amazing. He was engaging and kind to this shy 13-year-old farm girl from western Washington. We took pictures and had lunch just off the set. Then my uncle took me back to my parents.

All the scuffling in the car with my little brother on that long road trip was worth it to get to meet one of the all-time greats. The Duke will always be my hero.

Linda L. Shook Lakewood, WA

Getting her photo taken with a real-life celebrity like John Wayne dissolved any problems Linda had with her little brother.

JOHN WAYNE: GERALD FRENCH/GETTY IMAGES

The Talented Twins

My twin sister, Diana Jones, survived the eruption of Vesuvius in Pompeii, just not in A.D. 79. Diana and a young boy were carried to safety in the arms of actor Preston Foster in the 1935 movie *The Last Days of Pompeii*. She and I were movie extras in the '30s and '40s. Most notably, we were Meg's twins in the 1933 version of *Little Women*, starring Katharine Hepburn. For a brief time, the movie was shown in color on TV. It was fun to see ourselves dressed in pretty pink dresses instead of movie gray.

Babette Woodruff Leasure Prescott Valley, AZ

WATCHING THE SUNDAY MORNING FUNNIES

Comics read aloud on TV program spark the imaginations of these two boys.

Tom and his little brother John were serious about watching comics read.

When something went wrong with our TV, such as the picture flickering up and down, my dad pulled out the tubes and took them to the drugstore to test them in a contraption to see if they had to be replaced.

He wanted to keep the TV working because my brother John and I loved to watch a man read the Sunday morning comics aloud from the Milwaukee paper. The reader was on one of the three channels our TV picked up. He always read the comics slowly and deliberately, so we could follow every word and study the pictures: "And here Dagwood said to Blondie…"

My favorite was *Flash Gordon*. I even had a Flash Gordon ray gun and walked around the house shooting everyone, making *zing, zing, ba-zing* sounds. I thought it would be great to fly around in a spaceship like Flash, but when we went to the state fair, I was terrified of a ride called the Hurricane. You sat in a little spaceship and spun around at what I think was 2,000 mph. I decided I wouldn't be a good space rocket pilot.

The only bad thing about listening to the day's comics was that sometimes when I went to bed on Sunday night, I lay awake in the dark, hoping Ming the Merciless would not invade Earth. He never did.

Tom Mollica West Milwaukee, WI

SHARK!

In 1975, a horror film directed by Steven Spielberg filled movie theaters and emptied beaches. More than 40 years later, *Jaws* still fills us with frightening — and wonderful — memories.

I wasn't sure my 7-year-old could handle seeing *Jaws*, so before every scary scene, I'd put my arm around his shoulders to comfort him. During one tense scene, my arm jerked, practically pulling his neck off. When the next scary part was about to play out, he stopped me before I could wrap my arm around his shoulders again, assuring me that he was fine.
Candice Dunlap Peralta, NM

I was 7 when I saw *Jaws*. At the time, I didn't realize just how scary it was because I spent a good part of the film with my father's hand covering my eyes.
Maryann Lockwood Ringwood, NJ

My cousin Wendy and I were 13 when we saw *Jaws*. I don't know what our mothers were thinking, letting us go alone. Years later, we were both still afraid to go into the water.
Mary Wiswell West Winfield, NY

I was 15 when *Jaws* came out. I had my learner's permit, but to drive anywhere, I had to be accompanied by a licensed driver. Neither Mom nor Dad wanted to see *Jaws*, so my 65-year-old Irish grandmother agreed to go. All through the movie, she sat hunched down in her seat with her hands over her eyes. But every time that *da-DUM* started in, she peeked out between her fingers and squealed like a schoolgirl. Then she'd laugh uproariously! It's just one of a hundred great memories I have of my beloved Maw Maw.
Steve Johnson Ardmore, AL

Composer John Williams said that Spielberg did not originally like the *Jaws* theme and laughed when he first heard it.

FROM ONE CHILD TO ANOTHER

Sharing the joyful magic of movies through the generations.

The first movie I saw in a theater was *The Empire Strikes Back* in 1980, when I was 5. We saw it at the Starlite Drive-In indoor/outdoor theater in my hometown of Roseburg, Oregon. I was supposed to nap before we went, but I was too excited to sleep.

There was a very long line to get into the theater. A guy dressed as Lando Calrissian (administrator of Cloud City in the story) was standing at the front, greeting everyone as they came in. At one point my mom took my 7-year-old sister, Mary, and me out to the lobby for popcorn—and Darth Vader came and ate it with us.

My siblings and I grew up loving all the *Star Wars* movies, and we still love the movies to this day. I don't have children, but my siblings have passed on their love of *Star Wars* to their kids.

So in our family, *Star Wars* is definitely a series for all ages and generations.

Rayna Gausnell Roseburg, OR

Darth Vader, one of film's most memorable villains, is played by two actors in the early movies. James Earl Jones does the voice; David Prowse, a 6-foot-5-inch British bodybuilder and trainer, does the physical acting. The two haven't met.

Family Force

When *Star Wars* opened in 1977, we had never seen anything like it. We took our children to see it, and it will always be my personal favorite. In the years that followed, I introduced the series to my grandsons and took them to see the latest films in the theater. We went as a group to see *The Force Awakens* in 2015, something we continued to do with all the films in the series. As you can see (at right), Boba Fett is my favorite villain.
Kathleen Bowers Warren, MI

EXPLOSIONS AND MORE EXPLOSIONS!

So much excitement for this moviegoer in only the first five minutes.

No movie experience I've had has ever matched the one I had as a 10-year-old boy. It was the summer of 1977, and I went with my mother and sister to see some new movie called *Star Wars*, described as a "space opera." The theater lights dimmed, and after the introduction and thunderous music, the screen was filled with laser beams and explosions, spaceships, robots, troopers in white body armor shooting lasers, more explosions, and a princess— and that was just the first five minutes. Then Darth Vader made his appearance. To this day my mom swears I didn't blink or breathe until the end credits rolled.

Things we take for granted today—aliens, strange planets, lasers, space battles—were all new to my amazed eyes. *Star Wars* spoke to the kid in all of us, and that kid is still with me today. Thank you, George Lucas!
Martin R. Zdziemborsky
Gulfport, MS

Film editor Bruce Schoengarth is caught in rare moments in front of the camera—with William Shatner (Captain Kirk), who autographed the picture, and with Marianna Hill, who played psychiatrist Dr. Helen Noel in the first-season episode "Dagger of the Mind."

NOT JUST ANY JOB

Proudly helping out the crew of the
USS *Enterprise* behind the scenes.

My dad, Bruce W. Schoengarth, was a film editor for 14 episodes of the original *Star Trek*. Dad's time on the show is one of my claims to fame—it always turns a head when I tell someone!

In those pre-computer days, Dad's job was to take all of the film that had been shot, sit over an editing machine and weave it into a flawless one-hour show (minus commercial breaks). It took

great skill, technique and patience—and a very strong back.

Often during vacations and summer breaks, my siblings and I got to spend days at Paramount Studios while our father worked. I was able to "look out into space" from the bridge of the USS *Enterprise*, visit the captain's quarters and meet the actors, including Leonard Nimoy.

I still have the letter *Star Trek* creator and executive producer Gene Roddenberry wrote to my dad, dated March 14, 1967, inviting him to return to the crew for the second season.

Roddenberry even sponsored my parents' bowling team one year; everyone wore shirts with a picture of the *Enterprise* on the back!

Scott Schoengarth Olympia, WA

THE MUSIC GOES 'ROUND AND 'ROUND

Old song brings back happiness of youth.

We always had music in our home thanks to my daddy, Ted Schueller. The first song I remember is "The Music Goes 'Round and 'Round," published in 1935. Tommy Dorsey released a recording of the song in 1936 with vocalist Edythe Wright.

Ella Fitzgerald and others also recorded it, and Danny Kaye and Susan Gordon sang it in the 1959 movie *The Five Pennies*. But it was Dorsey's version that I first heard and still remember.

Thank goodness for YouTube! You can hear all those versions and more there.

JoAnn Schueller Cooke Prescott, AZ

A DATE WITH HERMAN AND HER BROTHER

Big fan didn't let anything stop her from having a blast at concert.

I was a huge fan of Herman's Hermits, and I wanted to go to California's Anaheim Convention Center in 1967 to see them play. Because I was only 15, my mom wouldn't let me go alone, so my brother Don went with me.

Don and I ended up sitting across the aisle from the only girl in the audience who was a screamer. She didn't listen to the music—all she did was scream. She tried to take a photo of the band, but her camera broke, and that made her scream and cry even more. I couldn't help feeling sorry for her, but I didn't allow her to spoil the music for me.

I still consider it one of the best concerts I have ever seen, even though I did have to date my brother.

Jan Cross Henderson, NV

GOING TO SEE THE ROCKET MAN

Expectations met and exceeded, thanks to his cool mom.

In 1976, when I was 12, I begged my parents to take me to the Elton John concert at the coliseum in Charlotte, North Carolina. My mom gave in. She arranged for a large group of family and friends to go with us, including my best friend and my sister and her best friend.

The performance was electric and powerful. I couldn't get over the piano, with its flashing lights around the perimeter that kept time with the beat of each song. The show, the theater, the band and Elton John were unbelievable—the sound was so much grander than what came out of my record player.

My mom officially became the coolest mom in the world. I will never forget that night.
Eric Hancock Concord, NC

All in the Family
This picture from 1958 reminds me of how our careers started. My dad, Pott Folse (accordion), still performs; brother Rick (sax) plays nine instruments; Ronnie (trumpet) plays keyboard; and Steve (trombone) is a drummer. I am the one playing the banjo. I was a singer for 35 years.
Debra Chiasson Raceland, LA

On with the Show

A day at the circus museum sure beats the heat of farm chores.

My mother, father and I took a day trip to Baraboo, Wisconsin, the original home of the Ringling brothers, in early July 1959. We were living on a dairy farm outside Fort Atkinson, and this was one of those rare days when my father could get away from his chores.

Circus World Museum, a tribute to Ringling Bros. and Barnum & Bailey Circus, had just opened, and the movie *The Big Circus* was premiering at the Al. Ringling Theatre. Rhonda Fleming and several other stars in the film were scheduled to attend the premiere. I was 15, and the thought of seeing a movie star up close was really exciting.

We arrived in the morning and saw all the memorabilia of bygone circus parades, and in the afternoon we went to the movie premiere. There she was, Rhonda Fleming, with her red hair and blue polka-dot dress, standing just a few feet away from me signing autographs. That was one of the high points of my life.

Fast-forward 58 years to May 2017, when Ringling Bros. and Barnum & Bailey Circus held its final performance. The museum in Baraboo is still open, though, and has added more circus treasures. But I'll always remember that special summer day in 1959.

Sharon Moe Furl Rio Rancho, NM

There she was, Rhonda Fleming, with her red hair and blue polka-dot dress, standing just a few feet away from me . . .

AUNT ELLA WAS THE FAT LADY

Being part of a sideshow act makes for many family stories.

My Aunt Ella was the final sideshow "fat lady" of the Ringling Bros. and Barnum & Bailey circus. Ella Grahn "Mills" Milbauer joined in 1956, replacing the circus's longtime fat lady, Alice from Dallas.

Aunt Ella's first year as a sideshow fat lady was quite an experience for a small-town Wisconsin girl. Having 17 various attractions, the 1956 Ringling sideshow was one of the largest. Admission to the sideshow was 50 cents, and Ella's husband served as one of the ticket takers. Billed as "586 Pounds of Feminine Charm," Aunt Ella made most of her sideshow money from selling "pitch cards" or photographs of herself.

A lifelong seamstress, Aunt Ella sewed all her sideshow gowns in bright colors, adding more fabric and gathers to make herself look even larger. Aunt Ella gave some gowns to my mother, thinking they could be used to make dance dresses for me. Instead, my brother and I used them as tents!

Aunt Ella eventually sought other sideshow opportunities, retiring from the Clyde Beatty-Cole Bros. Circus in 1961. She continued to be seen onstage as a special guest in a local community musical in Montello, Wisconsin.

One of my favorite stories: On my aunt's first circus trip, a robber broke into her trailer one night. Aunt Ella pushed the robber down and sat on him while Uncle Bob got the local authorities. Because clothing was hard for her to get on and off, my aunt slept in the nude. When the authorities arrived, they found a naked 600-pound lady sitting on the thief. I'd love to see that police report!
Pat Grahn Ripon, WI

Pat Grahn's Aunt Ella said of her sideshow cohorts: "It took a while to find out they were fine and friendly folks just like everyone else."

LEROY THE WIZARD

Growing up is full of excitement when your dad's a magician.

Unlike other people's houses painted white, my house was painted red and black and rolled on four wheels. Outside my bedroom window, I heard strange loud noises and people laughing every night.

One rainy day when I was 4, my mother told me to go with the red-haired lady babysitting me. We entered a very large building where hundreds of people were anxiously awaiting something. Suddenly, I heard a clash of cymbals accompanied by a drumroll. Out of nowhere, a man dressed in a tall black hat and a black suit with long tails appeared with a beautiful lady wearing a sparkling purple evening gown. I was shocked

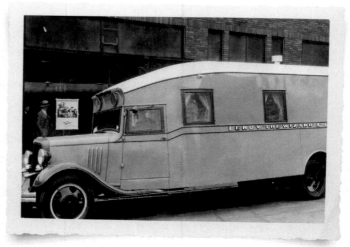

to realize these two elegant people were none other than my mother and father!

My father placed my mother in an adult-sized box and began pushing long silver swords in the holes. I could hear my mother screaming. A few

moments later, my father opened the door of this horrible box, and my mother gracefully stepped out of it, smiling! I raced backstage yelling, "Mommy! Mommy!" I wanted to be assured she was all right.

It was that day that I finally understood why I always heard people laughing outside my bedroom window. I now knew the other strange sound I'd heard from birth was applause! This was my introduction to the art of legerdemain (magical illusions) and show business.
Shirley Lavins Lyon Gaylesville, AL

The family's "house car" (above) rolling into town meant only one thing: Magic had arrived. An old theater in Colorado suited the sights and sounds of Leroy the Wizard & Co. in 1944.

Corrine (far left and above) tuned in to *Your Hit Parade* in the family car with her sister (at right in center photo).

Dancing in the Dark

With a little imagination, two sisters turn the family car into an entertainment center.

Our household radio was off-limits to everyone except Dad, who used it to listen to fights and daily market reports back in the 1930s. The radio's source of power, a car battery, was expensive to replace as well as to recharge.

Still, my sister Evelyn convinced Dad to let us listen to her favorite show, *Your Hit Parade*. Evelyn was going to high school and boarding with a teacher when she became a fan of the Saturday night radio program, which played the most popular tunes of the week, such as "Stardust" and "Smoke Gets in Your Eyes."

When she came home on weekends, Evelyn and I went to the garage every Saturday night, climbed into the front seat of the family car and turned the radio dial to *Your Hit Parade*. The garage was our home entertainment center. Each week we sat rooting for our favorite song to become No. 1.

In the winter we battled the frigid temperatures by heating four flatirons (normally used to iron clothing) and using them to warm our feet. Late in the afternoon, we'd pop a batch of popcorn, and at 7:45 p.m. we would wrap the hot flatirons in newspaper, bundle up and set out for the garage. Those days of making do with what we had formed lasting memories for Evelyn and me.

As I sit here all these years later, I am watching a program called *Dancing with the Stars* on a plasma TV in a house with central heating and air conditioning, and on the table next to my chair is a bowl of microwave popcorn.

Tonight they are dancing to the song "Begin the Beguine," and my mind returns to the simpler times I shared with my sister, swaying and singing together in the front seat of our family car.

Corrine Kautzman Kansas City, MO

Forever a Fan

For my brother Bill, football was life. Growing up in the small mining town of Peckville, Pennsylvania, Bill picked up a football in grade school and never put it down. He played through high school, and he won a full football scholarship to Albright College in Pennsylvania, where he played until he graduated in 1951. Then Bill joined the Marines and played three more years. He made his lifelong dream come true when he joined the NFL. Today, Bill is still a football fan. He never misses a chance to watch a game.

Peggy Krohto Skiver Portland, OR

Play Ball!

Junior baseball was a family affair. Among these charged fans, I'm seated (top row, far right) next to my sister and mother. Dad coached the team. My brother Larry played shortstop, while my little brother John was batboy. My sister Janie and I were often in the stands, and I had my share of crushes on Dad's star players.

Jackie Huetter

All Smiles in the Locker Room

The Bulldogs football team of Dugger, Indiana, had just defeated Clinton, our archrivals. The year was 1949. Our team went on to win eight games with only one defeat. We were a happy bunch when this picture was taken in the locker room right after the game. I am on the far right, with the striped T-shirt, and my brother Don is next to me with his hand on my shoulder. Our dad is behind me. He came to all of our games. I'll never forget how he cheered for us.
Richard Hiatt Atkinson, IL

Nothing Quite Like Being There

This is my little brother, George, and heavyweight champion Max Schmeling. In 1930, Schmeling was training in nearby Endicott, New York. The papers were full of descriptions of his routines, so we talked Dad into taking us to see the training camp. We watched, fascinated by the shuffling, snorting and punching men. Schmeling came out to greet the crowd, and I hauled out my trusty Brownie camera and snapped this photo. It was a great moment for us. On June 12, 1930, Schmeling won the heavyweight crown.
David Evans

GROWING UP IN THE HOUSE THAT RUTH BUILT

The joy of being a die-hard fan for decades.

From 1923 to 2008, the old Yankee Stadium was home to what I believe is the greatest sports franchise in the United States, the New York Yankees.

I first set foot in the House that Ruth Built in 1961, when I was 10, and my father took me to a doubleheader against the Chicago White Sox. I saw all my heroes: Mickey Mantle, Yogi Berra, Moose Skowron, Bobby Richardson, Tony Kubek, Clete Boyer, Roger Maris, Elston Howard and Whitey Ford.

Best of all, I got to spend the whole day with Dad, a true baseball fan. Living in New Jersey, I tried to go to as many Yankee games as I could.

One that sticks in my memory was in 1964. Dad got tickets for box seats right at field level, where we could reach over and pick up a foul ball. That day he took my sister Frances, my cousin Russell and me to see our Bronx Bombers play the Los Angeles Angels. I got a picture with Jimmy Piersall, who played for the Angels.

Those were the best seats I ever had at that stadium.

In 1966, I went with two friends to see the Yankees play the Minnesota Twins. We were all 14, and we took the bus from New Jersey to New York City, then the subway to the Bronx to see the game. We came back home the same way. All this, by ourselves; that would never happen today.

After the stadium was renovated in 1976, a junkyard in Connecticut was selling pairs of Yankee Stadium seats for $100. I bought some, and kept them until 2017, when I gave them to my niece Michelle and her husband, Colin, also loyal Yankee fans.

I continued to go to games to support my Yankees in the 1970s, '80s, '90s and 2000s. And I was fortunate to be at the last game ever played in the old Yankee Stadium on Sept. 21, 2008.

Topping off my devotion to the team and the stadium, I befriended Yogi Berra in 1996 and got to meet many of my old childhood heroes, along with more recent players.

The new Yankee Stadium is great, but going to the original with Dad will always have a special place in my heart.
Russell Marchetta Nokomis, FL

Jimmy Piersall, center fielder for the Los Angeles Angels, posed for a picture with Russell before a game at Yankee Stadium on Sept. 16, 1964.

TAKE ME OUT TO THE BALLGAME

Cereal in the morning, candy bar at the game.

1937

BREAKFAST OF CHAMPIONS

This ad claims that Lefty Grove, along with many other ball-playing stars, ate a hearty "rib-sticking" whole-wheat breakfast of Wheaties, and you should, too.

1927

ONE-LETTER DIFFERENCE

Many believe the popular Baby Ruth candy bar to be named after the "Sultan of Swat," but according to the Curtiss Cancy Co., it was originally named for President Grover Cleveland's daughter Ruth.

"A Breakfast of Champions IS THE TOPS"

LEFTY GROVE
Major Leagues' Leading Pitcher for 7 Years

Tomorrow... At Home... or Restaurant
ASK FOR WHEATIES

And It's Tops With These Stars, Too . . . .

First in the field

Baby Ruth is the best "forward pass" in the game; it scores every time—and all the time! And it has the largest, most enthusiastic following of any candy in America.

Forty million people eat Baby Ruth with delight. Over five million bars are sold every day. Over $250,000 worth of nickels pass over the candy counters daily for this favorite confection.

Fits every taste—fit for any taste—Curtiss Baby Ruth.

CURTISS CANDY COMPANY
New York   CHICAGO   San Francisco
          Boston   Los Angeles

Baby Ruth   5¢

Mike and Mara have never regretted skipping work and school to see the Tigers during their epic 1984 season.

Fever Pitch

When his team is on a roll, he follows a different school of thought.

Ours was the perfect father-daughter outing that day, even though, technically, we shouldn't have been there at all.

In 1984, our beloved Detroit Tigers won their first nine games, then 35 of their first 40, and never looked back. They led the season from start to finish, finally beating San Diego in five games in the World Series.

My daughter Mara, 10 that season, got swept up in Tiger frenzy. We spent hours poring over the stats in the sports pages, discussing who might overtake our Motor City Bengals.

One spring day early in the season, the team was at home for an afternoon game and I suggested making a pilgrimage to Tiger Stadium. But it was a weekday, which meant school for Mara and work for me. Carol—wife, mother and moral compass of the family—didn't care for my plan. Carol is no killjoy, but she worried about setting a precedent; baseball, she argued, is not more important than education.

Mara and I talked up the father-daughter nature of the caper. Carol relented but refused to have any further part in the conspiracy. I called the school to say I was keeping Mara home because she was running a fever. Abandoning any pretense of responsible parenting, I hung up, looked at

Mara and said, "She's got a fever all right," and then we chimed in unison, "baaasebaaall fever!"

In our seats, waiting for the first pitch, the moment overwhelmed me. I was sitting with my daughter in Detroit's historic grande dame, engaged in a divine rite of passage—skipping work and school for a day at the ballpark.

Mara had an encyclopedic knowledge of players and their managers. About the fifth inning, the Tigers' starting pitcher was getting hit hard. As manager Sparky Anderson bounced out of the dugout to talk to him, Mara grabbed my sleeve. "Watch as he steps over the foul line." Sure enough, Sparky gingerly tiptoed across, being careful not to step on it. "Comes from his days in the minor leagues," Mara continued. "He had to shine his own shoes and didn't want to get chalk dust all over them."

Overhearing our exchange, the guy in front of us turned around with an approving smile.

My good friend Tim Hughes, who'd also skipped work to see the game, took our picture at the stadium. Today, it serves as our official portrait of a time when Michigan was beset by a particularly virulent fever—and one of the best days of my life.

Mike Ranville Charlotte, MI

SPECTATORS WITH SPECTACLES

Half frames were popular in 1964 when my future husband, Bill, and his parents
went to see the Milwaukee Braves. Bill and his stepmom, Jean, wear half rims,
while his dad, William, sticks with trusty full blacks with metal accents.

Mary McCluskey Colgate, WI

PRECIOUS PETS

Whether a dog, cat, horse or monkey, a pet can quickly become part of the family. Just take a look at these heartwarming accounts of lovable animals.

Perfect Companion

Injured horse finds new purpose joining young girl on adventures.

My family moved from our small farm to a ranch in southern Oregon in 1944. I was 4 and my sisters were 13 and 15. Soon after, they went away to boarding school, and I had no one—not even a neighbor—to play with.

My mother did her best to entertain me, but my parents were concerned I was lonely. So when the opportunity came up to buy a horse, Dad took advantage of it.

Sweet Nellie was a rodeo horse, but she was retired because of a leg injury. She'd been around adults most of her life, yet when we met, she seemed to somehow know immediately that we were going to be buddies.

My parents couldn't afford a saddle, so when I got on Sweet Nellie's bare back, I had to take hold of the reins and hang on. She liked to trot rather than gallop and that suited me just fine. My parents loved to watch as I bobbed up and down.

She was always alert and aware of me. Even when she decided the ride was over, she was careful. She'd start to gently trot, put her head down and stop—a bit abruptly—so that I could slide down her neck onto the pasture. She never dumped me anywhere but on a soft spot in the clover, and then she'd wait until I could get back on my feet. Sometimes I led her right over to a fence post and climbed onto her back again.

At milking time, Sweet Nellie herded the cows to the barn. On hot summer days when the cows were trying to stay cool in the shade of the brush and low-hanging trees, she didn't hesitate to round them up. If I was on her back, I'd end up with bruises and scratches from the branches as Sweet Nellie did her job.

She responded to all my affection and gently took apples from my small hand. My loneliness faded whenever we were together, roaming the paths and pastures of our ranch. No dog or cat was more loyal, dependable, trusting and protective than my Sweet Nellie.

Nancy K. Culver Puyallup, WA

Nancy was in need of a friend when her dad found a retired rodeo horse who was looking for the same thing.

Snowball sits up in his favorite pose (above) and celebrates the birthday of Annette's brother, Carmen, in style (right).

An Upstanding Pup

Their dog Snowball was an upright family member in more ways than one.

On a sunny afternoon in 1952, my older sister, Theresa, came home holding a puppy. We lived in Niles, Ohio, and the white fur ball that was curled up in Theresa's shirt had come from a neighbor's litter.

Mom wasn't too happy about the interloper. She considered indoor pets a threat to order and cleanliness, and now my sister was breaking one of her major rules. But Theresa; our younger brother, Carmen; and I argued that at 16, 11 and 13 years old, we were perfectly able to care for a pet. Dad, who was more of a softy, sided with us, and Mom realized we had her outnumbered.

We named our lovable newcomer Snowball. At first Mom just tolerated the little invader, but eventually she grew to love him just as much as we did.

Snowball was a good listener. He never begged for food, even though he ate the same things we did because we couldn't afford dog kibble. He especially liked joining us for spaghetti and meatballs on Sundays.

He also celebrated holidays with the rest of the family. Carmen made sure Snowball had a party hat on for birthdays and a necktie on for New Year's Eve. Snowball wore whatever Carmen put on him, always happy to join in the family fun.

But what really made Snowball special was the trick Carmen taught him: sitting up on his hind legs. At first he sat up in a corner for some support, but then our talented canine began sitting up anywhere and everywhere, on his own, for long periods.

Snowball astonished people on our family visits to Dairy Queen. He'd sit up in the backseat of the car and lick ice cream from a cone held between his two front paws. At picnics, he perched on his haunches to be fed sandwiches and have his picture taken.

In fact, Snowball was upstanding in every sense of the word. He was an honorable and beloved family member for 14 wonderful years.

Annette Kochera Brookfield, OH

KISSED BY A MONKEY!

Grandma surprises her grandkids and has the photos to prove it.

My grandkids and I have a tradition of playing a question game we made up. We write as many funny or strange questions as we can think of on small pieces of paper that we place in a bowl. Then each person draws a slip and has to answer the question.

Once I drew the question "Have you ever kissed a monkey?" I said, "Yes!" and the kids whooped out loud. I had to tell them my story because they didn't believe me.

When I was in my early 20s, my grandparents had two little monkeys, Roger and Suzy, as pets. I showed the kids pictures of my grandmother Pearl Chamness holding one of her precious pals. Their house in Dayton, Ohio, had a 20-foot cathedral ceiling in the living room, with a balcony that

looked down into it. Whenever the monkeys got loose, which happened a lot, they had a grand time jumping from the balcony to the chandelier that hung from the living room ceiling. Boy, would they make a mess! And what noise…they squealed while we were trying to catch them!

I'm sure this was one reason my grandparents kept the monkeys for only a year. The other reason was the constant attempt to keep their cages clean. It was a daily job — sometimes more — as they loved to splash in the water bowls, like young kids playing in a shallow pool. But I will always cherish these memories of my grandparents' most unusual pets.

D'Avril "Dee" Chamness Dayton, OH

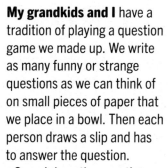

Pearl Chamness enjoys a quiet moment with her special simian friend.

FRISKY FRIEND

Unexpected find turns into something really special.

When I was 5 and playing with the neighbor boy, we suddenly heard noises coming from the sour-grape bush between our houses. Underneath was a scared little ball of fur that I convinced to come out of her hiding place.

I took this fur ball home and begged my mother to let me keep her. I came up with a name for her from the food bag: Friskie! It may not have been original, but as we would come to discover, it fit.

Friskie was a very pretty animal. Even guests who were not necessarily cat lovers commented on her appearance.

Her coloring was unique, and she had bright green eyes and little tufts of black fur that made her look similar to a Maine coon cat.

She became a wonderful pet and companion for me, and I loved her dearly. We had our own little games, like Touch the Tail: She was sensitive about her tail; when I would touch or stroke it, she would pretend it made her mad, but she always came back around for more.

She stayed away from passing cars and was a terrific hunter, always leaving us "presents' at the back door. I would sometimes catch her stalking her prey after dark. I was fascinated at just how quiet she could be, even keeping the two bells on her collar silent.

She would often accompany me on late-night walks. It m ght have been 2 a.m., but there would be ol' Friskie behind me
Richard Boettger Manor, TX

My mother, Jane Wilkinson, taught us a lot about compassion for animals. While growing up in Austin, Texas, we always had pets around—mostly dogs and cats. In this photo, taken around 1953, you can see how she provided kittens with a safe place to stay!
Tara Houghton Dorothy, NJ

Who's Thirsty?

During a family road trip that included a visit to the Seattle World's Fair in 1962, my grandparents' dog Duchess and I stopped at a fountain to rest. A blocked drain had caused the water to pool, so I invited my furry friend to drink with me. My mother—our trip photographer—thought we looked so cute that she snapped our picture, an all-time favorite of mine.
Sandra L. Hicks Sartell, MN

Alpine Buddies

There's no better companion for little Andred O'Connor on this snowy ski slope in 1965 than her gallant Saint Bernard, Chesty.

Prizewinning Pooch

Our beagle, Pebble, scored this trophy at a field trial in 1957. That's my father, Robert Rash, and brother Wayne sitting with our pup on the back porch. What a proud moment for us!

Linda Sprouse-Scott Midlothiar, VA

The Protector

Mother always said she was never afraid while Daddy was serving overseas in the Navy from 1943 to '46 because we had our precious dog, Spot, to protect us. He would be on the back steps every morning and wouldn't allow any strangers to come into the yard.

Jeanette Poehlmann
Brenham, TX

Best Lamb Around

Although our family lived in town, my parents let me keep a baby lamb in the tiny shed behind our house. I named him Jeepers after the song "Jeepers Creepers." One day while I was walking Jeepers around the neighborhood like a dog, I decided to go into the five-and-ten store. The owner, Mr. Harris, was known to watch children as they walked throughout the store. But he was so surprised at the sight of us that he just stood there. I'll never know why he allowed me to do it. I think it was because Jeepers was the most well-behaved lamb in town.
Necia Weinhold Lititz, PA

Adorable Times Two

The day we got my best pal, Spur, was so unexpected. We were walking past the pet store, and there was this collie pup that followed us all the way to the end of the glass in the front of the store. My mother said, "That must be our dog." He earned his name that very day. We got him on the "Spur" of the moment!
Robin Coffman Harlem, MT

Our patient pet lamb Tinkerbell was always willing to play
dress-up with my sisters and me. Teri (right), Jaci (center) and
I made Tinkerbell model outfits for holidays and special occasions;
I'm sure she loved all our fussing over her clothing selection.
We made her wear this ensemble—complete with a baby blue beret
to match my sisters' skirts—in 1964.
Toddi Darlington Thermopolis, WY

HOUND WAS SUCH A HAM

There was no other dog quite like good old Kim.

In July 1957, I had completed my four-year Air Force enlistment and received my discharge. Since I was both unmarried and unemployed, I moved back into my parents' home in Belmont, Massachusetts, to sort out my future. There I was reunited with Kim, a shepherd-collie cross who'd become a member of the family about a year before I left.

Upon my return, I found Kim to be a well-behaved mature dog who was a natural-born ham. My brother Bill and I enjoyed dressing her in costumes, and she seemed happy to participate. Shown here is one picture where she is dressed in my uniform, complete with cap, glasses and a cigar. She would hold the pose until we told her to resume her normal dog activities. She also played piano duets with my then-girlfriend, Dot.

Kim was an avid baseball fielder too. Bill and I would hit fungoes that Kim would catch with her mouth. I never could figure out why she didn't lose teeth.

In due time, Dot and I married and moved into our own no-pets apartment. This meant that my mother and Bill became the custodians of the dog.

Since that time, my wife and I have tried to raise other dogs, but there's been no replacement for good old Kim.
Norman W. Clark Holliston, MA

Class Clown

Jake stuck to me like glue and came to school with me every day. In 1950, my fifth-grade teacher tried to scare him away, but Jake always came back. Now my daughter, who is a teacher, takes her dog Sawyer to class. Today they call them therapy dogs. Jake and I were way ahead of our time.
Hazel Almendinger Johnstown, OH

Lifesaver

Bobo (below) was devoted to my older sister Kathryn and me. When I was a toddler, he kept me from falling into a brook. My father took this picture in 1953.
Dianne Bingham Stevens Hoosick Falls, NY

Copycat or Dog?

My sister Irma and our aunt's dog Tiger are yawning (above), but it's hard to tell who's the follower and who's the leader here. The photo was taken in the winter of 1953 in Richmond, California.
Clara Koussa Napa, CA

ALL-AROUND PALS

Lady guards two of her favorite humans, my sons Lars and Chris, at the family home in Eveleth, Minnesota. I rescued her as a pup in a remote Canadian village in the late 1960s.

George Erickson
Eveleth, MN

YOUR BEST FRIEND'S FOOD

Feeding only the choicest of options to Fido.

1974

WHICH IS WHICH?

Top Choice was a top seller for General Foods, along with its other pet brands Gaines-Burgers and Gravy Train. All said their dog food was like human food. "It even holds together like real hamburger," this ad says.

1959

ALL MEAT

Alpo, short for Allen Products Co., favored only canines in its ads through the 1950s and '60s. This one mentions that its food is "for dogs who are treated like members of the family."

1961

FURRY PITCH

Pet food marketing shifted in the '50s from depicting working animals, such as farm dogs, to more suburban pets worthy of pampering. Friskies' 1960s campaign had dogs in human hats, such as this spaniel in a baseball cap.

Top Choice® Burger on the left. Hamburger on the right. Or is it hamburger on the left and Top Choice on the right?

A wonderful change for your wonderful dog

ALPO
100% Chicken

Here's a wonderful flavor change! And, best of all, it's packed with the protein he needs for glowing health. Not a speck of starchy filler, it's all chicken. ALPO CHICKEN . . . for dogs who are treated like members of the family.

ALPO
Chicken
FOR DOGS

Like other members of your family, your dog needs meat. ALPO Beef or ALPO Horsemeat. ALPO Lamb, ALPO Chicken, ALPO Liver. All are 100% Meat. NEW: ALPO Meat Balls with Gravy! ALLEN PRODUCTS CO., ALLENTOWN, PA.

• • 116F

Meowy Christmas

This is my best friend, a sweet pussycat named Amber. She poses every Christmas as "Santa Claws" so we can send her photo to our many friends and relatives all over Canada.
Millie Dwyer Delta, BC

Holiday Bird

My pet turkey, Ruth, sat beside me when I was in the barn sprucing it up for Christmas, so I decided to decorate her for Christmas, too! Ruth did not mind the costume at all and seemed to enjoy the attention.
Kimberly Goodwin Chesapeake, VA

I'm pictured here (wearing headband) with my twin sister, Becky, meeting our furry friends in 1964. We had gone two long, sad months without a dog in our house and came home to find these adorable puppies, Bebe (left) and Buffy, waiting for us.

Bobbie Davenport Huntsville, AL

How Tall Are You?

One beautiful winter afternoon, my great-grandson Cameron was outside enjoying the new snow and playing with his Aunt Leslie's 4-year-old dog, Mattie. They played together for quite a while and then stopped to inspect each other. Cameron's mom, Emily, captured this shot.

Frances Smith Boiestown, NB

Snuggles in
December 1978
at 16 weeks
(above) and
at about nine
months (left).

Snuggles, the Sort-Of Brave Watchdog

All bark and no bite was definitely true of this schnauzer.

Some of our most joyous memories are of our schnauzer, whom we had named Snuggles since he was a real snuggler as a puppy. He was also a great watchdog…up to a point!

Once we were visiting my wife's folks, the Breedloves, in Aurora, Illinois, when a burglar tried to break in by climbing a ladder to the bedroom window. Snuggles barked, waking up everyone. My father-in-law sat up in bed, and the burglar was so startled, he backed down the ladder and fled the premises. Snuggles? We found him in the next room hiding under the bed to be safe!

Another time, I came home quietly to our big farmhouse in Leland, Illinois, and Snuggles failed to detect my entrance. I went up to the attic—my hideaway, where I often went to work on jigsaw puzzles and to just relax. Snuggles slowly became aware that someone was there and decided to investigate. He positioned himself in front of the attic door and began to growl. I ignored him, but the growling became much more intense, mixed with a couple of barks.

Finally, I decided to let him know it was just me, so I opened the attic door. Caught by surprise, our "brave watchdog" had all four feet going backward as fast as he could—down the hall and then three quarters of the way down the steps before he realized who I was. With his tail tucked between his legs and looking like a cat caught eating a canary, he slowly made it back up the steps to get scratched behind the ears—after I finally stopped laughing.

Donald P. Ames Indianapolis, IN

OUT FOR A STROLL

My husband and I were working in the yard on a brisk day in 1967 when our daughter,
Deb (right), and her friend Paula O'Conner came along pushing our dog Tippy in a stroller.
Tippy was a tad ornery 90% of the time, but to the girls he was just a doll.

Karen Chidester West Des Moines, IA

THE FAMILY CAR

Isn't it curious how these large objects designed to take us from points
A to B manage to find their way into our snapshots — and our hearts?

Runs in the Family

Bessy, the sturdy standby, has never let them down.

Before I was in my teens, this 1956 Ford Customline became a mainstay in our home. Our neighbor, Gaines Prater, owned a dealership in Calhoun, Georgia, where the car had been a demonstrator model. Mr. Prater drove it to our house, gave my dad the keys, quoted a price and suggested he drive it for a few days to see if he liked it.

Dad loved a bargain, but he wouldn't buy anything without careful evaluation. Mr. Prater knew his customers: He sensed it was time our family got a new car, and his low-pressure technique made the sale.

In the summer of 1965, my parents gave me the car for my sophomore year at Berry College. Then in 1966 Wanda and I started dating and used the car often. She liked my story of a favorite childhood blue bike I'd named Bessy, and soon Wanda gave that name to this car. We married that year. After we graduated, we took our daughter Agnes home from the Floyd Hospital birthing center in Bessy, which remained our primary vehicle until she was 17. Wanda says I know how to squeeze a penny.

Over the years, whenever a daily driver broke down, we'd pull out Bessy. It was this car that took me to my evening classes at grad school.

When our eldest granddaughter, Emily, was in high school, she and I woke Bessy from a 30-year hibernation and restored her. Emily drove the car to proms, to photo shoots and back to Berry, where she also attended.

Bessy's story is not over yet. But Emily is handling the next chapter.

Lester Brookshire Rome, GA

> When our eldest granddaughter, Emily, was in high school, she and I woke Bessy from a 30-year hibernation and restored her.

Still on a Roll

A member of the family for seven decades, this vintage Chevy remains his ride and joy.

Everyone in our neighborhood in Austin, Texas, wanted a ride in my mom's new 1951 Chevrolet DeLuxe. I was 8 years old when she got it. Now, about 70 years later, I'm driving that car, which is firmly entwined in our family history.

I learned a lot while driving in that Chevy with Mom, from hearing the truth about Santa Claus to watching integration protests in Texas. The car became mine when I graduated from high school in 1961 and Mom bought another Chevrolet. As a graduation present, my grandmother paid to have the green car repainted.

The Chevy took me off to college and then to med school in 1965 in Galveston, where it survived Hurricane Carla and yet another flood where water rose higher than the doors.

In 1966, I met a woman named Judy Lynne while preparing to enter the Peace Corps; on our dates, we drove the Chevy on ocean beaches. We got married in 1969, and the Chevy, of course, took us on a trip to Mexico in 1970.

Later, we moved to Chapel Hill, North Carolina, where our first child, Melanie, was born in 1975.

In 1981, Steven (above with his family and mom, Lilli) had owned the Chevy for 20 years already. In 2013, he and his wife, Judy, entered it in a car show.

She came home from the hospital in the Chevy on a hot summer day. Our second child, Jennifer, was born in 1978 in Louisville, Kentucky, and as we were bringing her home from the hospital during a fierce snowstorm, the Chevy got stuck in our driveway. Our third child, Michael, arrived on a spring day in 1981, and the Chevy sported new seat covers for his ride home.

Now my grandson, age 3, is interested in the car, which has never been restored. I hope he stays interested—I'd love to keep it in the family!

Steven Lippmann Louisville, KY

One Cool Ride

The red 1941 Plymouth Special Deluxe convertible my brother Hank bought new was a very cool car. So when he left home to join the U.S. Army Air Forces in 1942, you can imagine my reaction when he gave me the keys and said I could drive it while he was gone. I was about 18 years old, and I had a very good time with that car. As you can imagine, I thought I was the cat's meow driving around our little river town of Moscow, Ohio. When Hank came home in 1945, I had to give up the car. Wish I still had it today!

Anna Cushard Staats Tamarac, FL

Sweet 16

As soon as I turned 16 in 1963, I got my driver's license. My dad had taught me in our family's 1958 Chrysler. It was chartreuse green with enormous fin fenders. One of the first times I took it out by myself was to help my 10-year-old sister, Arnis, deliver May baskets. We drove to our first stop, and as I backed out of that driveway, one of the fancy fins hung up on a fire hydrant. It took three men and two car jacks to get it off. Here, Arnis and I stand with our mom, Jeanne Hunt, in front of the Chrysler in 1961.

Gayle Hunt Matz Brookings, SD

Uncle Maurice Anderson (with Aunt Wauneta in 1950 at a family reunion) loved his 1948 Plymouth, which he bought as car production rebounded after World War II. It was his pride and joy.

Robert Hornby Grand Island, NE

I snapped this cute shot of my daughters Diane and Helen asleep
in their winter coats in the back of our family's 1941 Ford after
a visit to their grandparents' house in the early 1950s.
David Reimer Windsor, ON

Cool at Any Speed

Between the ages of 16 and 18, I got 17 speeding tickets. Over the years I used my ticket experience to help young men understand that choices have consequences. One of those young men was my son Nate. When he was a teenager, Nate secretly planned with his mother to find me a '68 Camaro, the car I dreamed of as a young man. When they finally found one, my wife told me to check it out because "your son thinks you have suffered enough." Today, 20 years later, it is still a dream to drive. Is it fast? Yes. But I have not received one speeding ticket while driving it.
Sam Weirbach Redmond, WA

Dune Buggy Dream

My daughter Gail wasn't thrilled when I brought home a VW wreck to be her first car in 1968. But after I stripped it down and put a new Meyers Manx dune buggy body on it, Gail became a bit more enthused. We were living on California's Alameda Island, where her car was a big hit.
Roy Nichols Reno, NV

ROAD TRIP!

On our way to Minnesota in 1954, my dad, Jeff Weston, and my sister Ann looked stylish as they stretched their legs at a gas station.

Sue O'Neill Beatrice, NE

Earl with his dad's '68 Charger (left); the family with the '66 Mustang (below).

A FAMILY AFFAIR

Very persuasive son helps Dad make the right car decisions.

As a 16-year-old driver in Philadelphia, Pennsylvania, I urged my father to buy my mother and me a 1966 Ford Mustang. He did, and when Dodge came out with a redesigned '68 Charger, I persuaded him to buy that car, too. Occasionally, I was even allowed to drive it.

The Charger was a great car, with hideaway headlights, turn-signal indicators on the hood and unique styling. But to my dismay, my dad ordered it with hubcaps instead of rallye wheels.

Then one day in 1970, the unthinkable happened: My dad totaled the Charger. It turned out lucky for me, though, because he lent me its insurance settlement to buy a car of my own. I bought a 1970 Dodge Challenger— rallye wheels and all.

Earl Silverstein Eagle, ID

All Lined Up

From left to right: Brothers Bernie, Fritz, Bill, Bob and Alvin Jeske pose with their cars after returning from the Army in 1949. Four of the five went into trucking. The fifth became a plumber.

Orville Jeske Glenwood City, WI

Fast Flyer

In this May 1955 photo, I am sitting with my mother on my 1929 Ford pickup-converted-to-roadster. With this bright red hot rod, I took corners at 80 miles per hour! It looked funny, and the fenders shook when it idled, but it was the greatest car on the road.

Herbert Flowers San Diego, CA

A Coupe of a Different Color

That old girl was ready to paint the town.

Money was scarce around our house with a family of 12 during the Great Depression. My parents made sure we had plenty to eat and a roof over our heads, but if we wanted anything more than that, we had to pay for it ourselves.

My brother Frank was determined to get a car. So he worked in a grocery store every day after school and saved all his earnings for two years. By the time he turned 18, he had enough to buy his first car.

He was very proud of it and couldn't wait to show it off. With their first glance at it, my parents could feel their blood pressure soaring. It was a beat-up old coupe with a rumble seat and was in desperate need of a paint job. Having spent all his savings to buy the thing, Frank had no choice but to use paint left over from our bathroom and kitchen decorating—yellow and pink.

Mother had an anxiety attack whenever she looked at that yellow-and-pink eyesore parked in front of our house; the rest of us just tried to avoid the neighbors.

In spite of his car's paint job and condition, Frank always managed to get plenty of dates. I'm sure his good looks had something to do with it. And it helped that not many 18-year-olds had a car back then.

Occasionally Frank would double-date with a friend, but because there was room for only two in the cab, the other couple had to ride in the open-air rumble seat and take their chances with the weather. I remember watching the four of them drive off one fine summer night without a cloud in the sky. Minutes later, a sudden thunderstorm drenched the two unlucky people perched in back.

I still laugh about that car.

Martha Mahon Trenton, NJ

Road Revenge with a Feisty Coronet

Mom had a tipping point, and she wasn't shy in showing it.

In 1970, our mom, Sylvia, was the organist, pianist and choir director at our church in Cedar Grove, New Jersey, so we were in church every Sunday. On occasion, we'd stop at Dunkin' Donuts on our way home.

We had a 1966 Dodge Coronet 440, which had the largest standard engine for its make and model. The big white Dodge had black vinyl bench seats and no seat belts, which weren't mandatory until 1968. So if Mom made a sharp turn, we'd have to hold on to the rock-hard elbow rest on the door or we'd slide across the bench and wham against the opposite side.

Anyway, one Sunday, Mom had stopped at the doughnut store with my sisters, Kathryn and Emily, and me. As we were leaving, some guy cut us off when we turned right to go up the hill. That made Mom angry.

"Jimmy," she said, "I can't take this anymore." Then she floored it. The nose of the Dodge lifted about a foot in the air. My mom was 5 feet 2 inches and I was even shorter, so we couldn't see a thing over the dashboard for several seconds. Our car flew up the hill, blowing past the guy, until Mom, cursing in several languages, cut in front of him.

I was scared, but I was proud of my mother. To this day, I cannot fathom how she managed to steer when the front of the car rose off the ground.

Jim Lagergren Johnson City, TN

Our car flew up the hill, blowing past the guy, until Mom...cut in front of him.

Joined by their dog Ralph, siblings (from left) Kathryn, Emily and Jim await another car ride.

From Gremlin to Mermaid

One family takes a journey to pick up an aquamarine beauty.

July 3, 1980: I had just turned 9, and Mama, Papa, Granny, Aunt Fleury and I were going on a road trip from Trenton, New Jersey, to Carlinville, Illinois, to pick up our new car, a 1977 Buick Riviera.

Owned by my maternal uncle, Jose K. Villegas, this was no ordinary vehicle. It was a vibrant mermaid-fin aquamarine with a white vinyl roof, wood panels, a cornflower blue interior and an eight-track stereo.

The 889.7-mile, 13-hour-and-41-minute journey was a first for our 1973 AMC Gremlin. We headed down I-95 to Philadelphia, Pennsylvania, visiting the Liberty Bell, Independence Hall and the art museum. In Chinatown we ate "inside-out chicken wings" stuffed with shrimp and scallions.

At the St. Moritz Hotel in New York City, we met Aunt Estela and Uncle Paulino, visiting from the Philippines, and dined on dim sum at the historic Nom Wah Tea Parlor. Estela and Paulino then rented a car and joined us on the trip. Imagine a four-day slumber party of five giggling girls—Uncle Jose's daughters and me—jumping on beds. The adults reveled in Chicago's jazz clubs.

Was the car worth it? Well, after nearly 40 years, it's still in the family. Our blue angel has taken us to the Elks Club Antique Auto Show and to the Ewing Township Fourth of July parades in 2014 and 2015. I dress up to drive her, but I'm not sure who's getting more whistles.

She's a reminder of my '80s adolescence when cars were elegant alligators. Pretty in pink? More like Jersey girl of the aquamarine deep.

Leonora Rita V. Obed Ewing, NJ

MOTORING MEMORIES

New cars are always exciting, even these thrifty options.

1972

SMALL CAR, BIG SALES

Known for clever design, efficiency and low price, the Datsun was the top-selling import in 1975. The 1200, shown here, was a bestseller, with 89,000 sold between 1970 and 1973.

1950

WITH UPGRADES IN MIND

Studebaker's automatic hill-holder feature cost extra on this Champion four-door sedan model. It prevented the car from rolling back when uphill.

GP, the Automotive Pioneer

With Grandpa and his cars, family stories are aplenty.

My grandfather George Pollock McGraw—aka GP—had an incurable case of "car-itis." He proudly bought the very first car in Woodbury County, Iowa: a 1901 Rambler. No license was required at that time, but Iowa passed its motor vehicle law the next year, requiring a one-dollar fee. The secretary of state sent him his license plate, numbered 100, which we believe to be the first number in the state of Iowa. GP displayed it in the garage (see bottom right) along with others from the first 39 cars he owned in his lifetime. He was even once featured in a *Time* magazine article showcasing his unique collection.

In his free time, GP drove around a lot. He loved his car, and I suspect he delighted in showing it off. He began taking long road trips before the time of highways, gas stations and Starbucks. In those days, travel by automobile was always an adventure. On one trip, he and his son drove his Chalmers to Colorado and then to the top of Pikes Peak. They reported that the biggest problem was the strong wind threatening to blow them off the mountain! GP was issued the Pikes Peak Summit Motor Club certificate on August 13, 1921.

A favorite family story about GP centers around a wager. A car could not climb the highest hill in Iowa without a team of horses pulling it—but GP said his car could, so he crammed the Auburn's gearshift into reverse, stomped on the accelerator and raced backward up that pesky hill!

When I was about four years old, I finally got to ride in his Packard. GP and my father were in the front, where the view was good and the air seemed fresh, but I was in the backseat. "Here we go," GP said, and he lit up his cigar as we jackrabbited out of the driveway. The cigar smoke made me quite nauseated, so I baptized the backseat with vomit. He never asked me to go for a ride again.

If there are roadways in heaven, you can be sure GP is on one of them, preening inside a shiny new automobile!

Janeen A. Johnson Battle Ground, WA

GP's dapper suits made fine accompaniments to any of the many cars he owned.

BUILT FORD TOUGH

Dependable twin brothers and their dependable twin autos.

My favorite photograph from our family album shows my grandfather Arley Smith with his twin brother, Farley, proudly standing next to their Model T's. Like the brothers, the cars are virtually identical. The one-digit difference on the 1925 Indiana license plates is the only way to tell the vehicles apart.

Arley and Farley worked from sunup to sundown on their family farm in central Indiana. Like my ancestors, Henry Ford had a thorough understanding of the challenges of rural life. His mission was to design and manufacture an inexpensive and dependable workhorse for all Americans, and the Model T fit the bill perfectly.

The Smith boys look pretty dapper in their straw hats and Sunday suits. I can imagine my grandfather and great-uncle wiping the dust from the black lacquered fenders. I bet they gave a shine to the brass, too. In the sunlight, these tin lizzies must have looked pretty elegant.

David Ladd Cicero, IN

'39 Mercury Was One of Us

From one state to another, memories came along with this ride.

The family car was not something I thought much about—I just dutifully got into the vehicle when I was told. Still, it was quite a sight when Dad came home with a maroon '39 Mercury in 1940, much like the one in the photo. He drove it up the driveway to our farmhouse on the hill, grinning ear to ear. The car was almost new, and we'd never owned anything so nice before. I felt privileged, and that was an awesome feeling in the '40s!

Eventually, our family of four prepared to move to California—to the land where opportunities abounded and money would be a more ready commodity than it was in Kansas, or so that is what we thought.

When my parents packed for us to leave, the backseat was piled high with bedding, clothing, dishes, my sister's crib and anything else we could cram in. My baby sister and I lay on top of the bedding (no child seats back then!) as my dad drove us down Route 66 to the Golden State.

This car traveled with us to McFarland, California; to the coast where Dad later worked in a defense plant; again to McFarland; and finally back to the farm in Kansas. We moved home on Christmas Eve, and Dad cautiously navigated a snowstorm in Oklahoma until he saw the lights of a filling station and a little motel. My parents decided we would stay there for the night while he patched the tire one more time. We traveled on a wing and a prayer, but we made it.

Back on the farm, my father taught me to drive using the '39 Mercury. We went out to the wheat field, and I practiced turning, stopping and, of course, shifting. The cows watched from across the fence, quietly chewing their cud.

We still had the Mercury during my high school days. Someone had smashed into it, so you had to enter from the passenger's side. When I saw my cousins at my grandparents' house on Sundays, we would go riding, banged-in side and all. Finally, Dad saved up enough money to get the car fixed, and he also had it painted a gray color. He drove it to my wedding.

Doris Schroeder Hutchinson, KS

Coveted Car

My constant desire whenever we visited my grandparents in Elk County, Pennsylvania, was "to drive the little car." They rarely agreed, but on this sunny day in 1941, I got my wish. Here I am at the wheel with my cousins and my big sister Mary (with glasses).
Joan Wheeler Erie, PA

Hand-Me-Down

This 1965 Barracuda has been in our family for half a century. My dad was a Belvedere station-wagon-type person, but I somehow managed to persuade him to buy this two-door, V-8, compact, bucket-seat model for our family so that I could have the old family car when I got my license. After college, when the engine on my car failed, I got the Barracuda. It has become the most important object my father left me.
Ronald Weinger Berkeley Heights, NJ

HER CHEVY'S SECRET LIFE AS A HOT ROD

New car has a winning streak, thanks to son.

My mother, Bess Straughan, had just bought a new Chevy in 1955—and she was so proud of it. My brother Joe, who was 16 at the time, was itching to drive it. Mom was hesitant, but after a lengthy lecture about speed and making him promise not to leave the city limits or drive over 40 mph, she let him take her car for the evening.

Soon Joe was driving the Chevy regularly.

One day, Mom noticed the car was burning through oil.

She couldn't figure out what was causing the trouble, so she made an appointment for the dealer to check it out. Something was wrong, she was sure—the dealer was really going to hear from her.

The appointment was for a Monday. On the Saturday before, she drove to the grocery store. As she was walking out with her purchases, helped by one of the store's teenage clerks, he asked her which car was hers in the parking lot. Mom pointed to her aqua and cream Chevy.

"Wow," the clerk said. "Is that yours? That's the fastest car in town!"

Apparently, Joe had been taking Mom's Chevy out to a long stretch of Highway 32 where teenagers drag-raced. And it won most of the time.

That night, Mom canceled her appointment with the dealer. Joe's short-lived reign as a drag-race king ended abruptly.

Mary Chatman Puxico, MO

"Wow. Is that yours? That's the fastest car in town!"

A rev-elation: Mom didn't know her son was a lord of the blacktop in her beloved new car.

The trusty '49 Ford that Ann took over when she got her license sure was a sharp-looking ride.

Driving with Daddy

Getting his approval was the key.

These days, North Kickapoo Street in Shawnee, Oklahoma, is a four-lane road leading out to the interstate and is lined with all kinds of places to eat and shop. But in the mid-1950s, it was just a gravel country road—the perfect place for our daddies to teach us how to drive.

We didn't have driver's education at Shawnee High School. We were on our own. Mom took me to pick up an instruction manual. I was the oldest of my friends, so we were excited at the prospect of a whole new world opening up. We'd have freedom to get around. Best of all, we could go to the Starlite Drive-In theater on 50-cents-a-carload night. We'd have it made.

Mom let me back our 1949 Ford out of the garage a few times to get used to the clutch and gearshift. I got familiar with the motion but was hardly ready for my road test.

Finally, the day came for Daddy to give me a real lesson. He drove out to the end of the paved section of Kickapoo Street and across to where the gravel started. My daddy had come from a family

of 10, and they had been farmers in Oklahoma during the Dust Bowl. There was only one way to do things, and that was the right way.

Compliments were rare, so when he muttered his approval, it was special. I didn't want to experience his glare if I ground the clutch or if the car jerked as I tried to get it going.

I took a deep breath, slowly let out the clutch, pushed the stick into second gear, eased down the road and then carefully moved into third gear. He had me stop and repeat the procedure two or three more times until I came to the end of the section. I was feeling pretty good as I came to a stop and looked to Daddy for approval.

He glared at me and then barked, "You've been driving, haven't you?"

He must have thought I'd been practicing in somebody else's car. I quickly explained that my training was all on the up and up.

That was so many years ago. I can still see the nod he gave me when he said, "Well, you did good."

Ann McDonald Shawnee, OK

Going through a car wash with an open top is definitely an adventure. These ladies don't look phased by it.

First Time Through the Car Wash

Mom had a good, clean sense of humor for sure.

When I was young, my mother owned a yellow Jeepster that she nicknamed the Little Hornet. One afternoon, as we were driving home from my school, we stopped at a light, and a huge truck with slatted sides pulled alongside us. The wind blew an undeniable stink into the hot air, but the truck seemed to be sheltering us. Then a loud mooing sound came from Mom's side of the car.

The combination clicked into place like a precision clock striking the hour: loud cow noises, strong wind, open slats on the truck and, inevitably, a release of slimy cow dung raining into the Hornet. The light turned green, and the truck went on its way, but we just sat there.

Finally, my mother started to laugh. She put the car in gear and headed straight to the car wash.

When we got there, she positioned the Jeepster on the rails, and we moved toward the automatic sprayers. I couldn't believe we weren't getting out, so I closed my eyes and held my nose as the soap squirted from a line of nozzles.

The water started, and a big blue curtain began to slap at the hood of the car. "Lie down on the seat," yelled Mom.

Soon we were soaking wet and being hit by long foam strips that passed quickly overhead.

For the next five minutes, we dodged the rollers, straps, flaps, soap and water. When the sprayers started, Mom yelled, "Close your eyes and sit up."

The cool water felt so good in the heat, and the stinky mess was washing off. I got soap in my mouth, but we were mostly clean, and so was the Hornet.

As we exited, the blowers dried us off. We opened the doors; most of the water was gone, with the floor drain taking care of the rest. I looked at my mother, and her hair was a crazy mess, stiff as a board. She looked at me, pointed and started to laugh. Everyone at the car wash was applauding. Heads held high and stiff witch hair blowing in the breeze, we left for home to explain our day to Dad.

Patti Miller Stammer McKinleyville, CA

THEN

NOW

GEARHEADS

In 1964, my father and three of his brothers were working on a car in the driveway. My grandma, who always had her camera ready, snapped a shot. Fifty years later, the Hovan boys re-created the picture! From left to right: Bill Hovan, Robert Hovan (my dad), Joe Hovan and — taking the place of Uncle Jack, who passed away — my Uncle Andy.

Doug Hovan Berea, OH

VACATION TIME!

Whether going on a cross-country camping adventure, taking a trip to the world's fair, visiting Yellowstone or touring Disneyland, traveling with family is the way to go.

At the rim of the Grand Canyon in Arizona, David took a photo of his parents and sister Debra.

Taking the Long Way Home

In the days before cellphones, credit cards and GPS, travel truly was full of the unexpected.

My husband, Bob, had just completed 10 months of schooling in June 1969 at Fort Bliss, El Paso, Texas, and we were packing for our return trip to Rhode Island with our children, David, 7, and Debra, 6. Bob had a few weeks before starting a new job, so we decided to drive first to the West Coast and then head back home.

We wrote down what we wanted to see along the way, shared the list with AAA and they mapped out a route for us. We bought some traveler's checks and I faithfully wrote in our travel diary every day.

We had a roomy Chevy Impala that had no seat belts. Debra liked to read, so she arranged herself on the floor in the back and David had the whole seat to himself. We packed little gifts to amuse the children along the way—things like coloring books, games and sticker books.

Stopping in Tombstone, Arizona, we got to see the town and the history that went with it, and then we drove through a hailstorm in Yosemite National Park. In Las Vegas, Bob and I wanted to stop and see Bob Newhart and Teresa Brewer, but I wondered what to do with the children.

"Don't worry," Bob said. "They have bonded babysitters and if anything happens to the children, we will get paid." Reluctantly I gave in, and all went well.

After 23 days of traveling with two children in tow, I will always have fond memories of that trip.

David and Debra saw the Earp brothers in Tombstone, Arizona, and Pluto at Disneyland in California.

Bob wanted to stay the night in Wells, Nevada, so we could see the salt flats during the day, but there were no rooms available anywhere. We hadn't made reservations in advance because we didn't want the pressure of getting to a certain place by a set time.

So we continued driving to Salt Lake City. Again, no rooms—a big convention was in town. Finally, around 2 a.m. we pulled into Ogden, Utah, and booked the bridal suite with its queen-size bed. The couple who had reserved it never showed up.

Going through Wyoming, we descended from 9,000 feet through a cloud. We saw Mount Rushmore and Wall Drug. In Baraboo, Wisconsin, we saw Circus World. Heading east we took the car ferry across Lake Michigan. Our final day included Niagara Falls.

After 23 days of traveling with two children in tow, I will always have fond memories of that trip.

Roberta Godin Mystic, CT

Matterhorn Family Photo

This shot was taken on the Carousel of Progress in 1970, during one of our yearly trips to Disneyland! From left, that's me, my dad, my sister Debbie, my Grandpa Albert and family friend Teri.
Mark Villwock Correy
North Tustin, CA

Pluto and Plaid

Here are my three sons (below) at the Disneyland gates in 1974. Gasoline was rationed, so we had to ride the train to California from Seattle. Once we got there, Christopher (left) walked so much, he wore holes in his pants cuffs!
Carla Forgey Seattle, WA

Ready to Ride

My grandparents would take us to Disneyland whenever my family visited them in California. This photo from 1962 or '63 shows my sister Kathy (above in curlers) riding Dumbo with me. Why anyone would wear curlers on Dumbo, I don't know.
Linda Hankla Clearwater, NE

The highlight of 1957 for me was winning a trip to Disneyland.
My family, from left, mother Helen, sister Jill, father Guy and
I flew from Nebraska to experience the happiest place on earth.
Judy Phipps Sipe Tustin, CA

MORE SURPRISES THAN THEY BARGAINED FOR

An unforgettable road trip to Colorado for a family of six.

We were excited in 1967 for our first real family vacation from Missouri to Colorado. We had a brand-new 1966 station wagon, which had enough room for all six of us and our suitcases. Our children were 4, 9, 11 and 13—old enough for a 600-mile road trip.

We left early on a Sunday morning and hoped to reach Golden, Colorado, by 5 p.m. We stopped for lunch around 1 p.m. and had just gotten back on the road when— *BANG!*—a tire blew out. My husband, Leroy, changed the tire, but we were still 200 miles outside of Denver and nervous about going on without a spare. Money was tight: We'd budgeted very carefully for a six-day trip, and there was nothing left over for a new tire. And we had only one credit card, a Montgomery Ward charge card. Wonder of wonders, at a nearby mall, we found a Montgomery Ward store.

Once in Golden, with a new spare, we spent the week exploring the area in and around Rocky Mountain National Park. We hiked trails, rode the tram in Estes Park and climbed a fire tower to look out over the Rockies. At the top of Mount Evans, the kids were amazed to run into a snowstorm in August. And I was shocked to run into the doctor who had set my broken arm back in Missouri when I was 11!

But the biggest surprise of all came as we were driving home. With about 250 miles to go—*BANG!*—another blowout. We managed to make it home, slowly, all of us with our fingers crossed the rest of the way.

None of us has ever forgotten that trip. Even our youngest, John, who was only 4 at the time, swears he remembers it.
Irene Worley Savannah, MO

The Worleys take a breather after hikes in the Rockies in 1967.

FISH OR FOUL?

Parents knew how to plan a good time for all.

While stationed at Williams Air Force Base in Arizona, my husband, Fred, and I often drove our 1960s Plymouth station wagon to Water Dog, a recreational area in the mountains near Roosevelt Lake. We would fold down the back seats, slide a mattress in place and load up our five children while they slept. When we arrived, Fred and the kids would go fishing for our dinner. One time we left the pan of grease from the fried fish outside. Later we found a family of skunks scarfing it up—fish bits and all. In the photo at left, daughter Lori, 5, sits on the car's tail end.

Charlotte Richards Sumner, WA

'CRACKING UP' THE KIDS

The Jolly Green Giant has done it again.

The lure of summer asphalt in 2006 found me in a car with, at right, two teenagers—my son Mark, 13, and niece Amanda, 16—and Spencer, my wired 7-year-old. We traveled west from Milwaukee, through Nebraska and South Dakota, to see Chimney Rock, Mount Rushmore and the Crazy Horse monument.

On the drive home, we hit the Spam Museum and Blue Earth, Minnesota, a town sporting a 55-foot-tall Jolly Green Giant statue. Gazing up, Mark commented, "He's got mold in his crack." The kids reeled, laughing, while I chuckled and shook my head. Being both the mom and chauffeur on a classic American road trip had its moments.

June Groshek-Czarnezki
South Milwaukee, WI

Beach Pose

I'm the one tilting my head in delight at the warm surf of Daytona Beach, Florida, in 1955. With me are my mother, Marguerite (at left), Aunt Mary and my sister Carol.
Joanne Moore Yuma, AZ

Cool at Last

My Grandmother Dana and Great-Aunt Vasa joined us for our summer trip from Milwaukee, Wisconsin, to Sarasota, Florida, in the 1970s. We crammed into our VW wagon, that had no air conditioning, and my grandmother refused to open a window because she'd had her hair set. Relief came at a motel in Tallahassee when we jumped into the pool. From left: my mother, Mira, Susan, Dana and Vasa.
Christina Spalatin Wauwatosa, WI

Sunny Day

My family has vacationed at the same spot on Cape Cod in Massachusetts since 1952! Here I am (far left) with my brothers Peter (center) and Gary and mother, Loretta, in 1961.
John Hawkins Mequon, WI

Live Reptiles

Alligators in fenced-in pits once gave rides to kids at the California Alligator Farm. Located across the street from Knott's Berry Farm in Buena Park, California, the Alligator Farm also housed turtles, ostriches and snakes. My grandparents Margie and Jess Doty stand by as Billy the gator provides a seat for my brother Dennis and me.
Genene Doty Staats Agua Dulce, CA

Racers try to set speed records at Utah's Bonneville Salt Flats, where Ellen and her parents (inset) stopped on their way to California.

Slipping Through the Sands

A photo-op on their 1963 road trip comes to a messy end.

My father thoroughly believed in long vacations. Time off always meant going somewhere. In the summer of 1963, we drove our AMC Rambler from Maine to California. We would be gone for a month and intended to see as much of the country as possible.

We took great care in crafting the itinerary. Most of the stops were designed to entertain my mother and me, but Daddy's one must-see was the Bonneville Salt Flats in Utah.

For a hundred years, racers have tested the limits of their vehicles on this smooth, flat surface that by summer's end is as hard as concrete and ideal for racing. In 1914, Teddy Tetzlaff was one of the first to set a land speed record here, recording 142.8 mph in a Blitzen Benz.

The flats are on the western edge of the Great Salt Lake basin, and that part of Utah is hot, but in the summer of 1963 it was even hotter than usual. The sweltering weather overwhelmed us before we reached the famous testing grounds.

When we arrived, Daddy wanted a picture of Mama standing in the vastness of the testing grounds. He told her to walk onto the salt flats so he could get the photo without the line of fencing behind her.

When Mama hesitated, he assured her and said, "It's fine. They race cars on this stuff."

Less than 50 feet off the road, the salt crust did the inevitable and gave way. Mama's face said *I told you so!* better than words as she sank up to her knees in some of the vilest mud on earth.

I screamed that Mama was going to go under, and Daddy could only dance back and forth in indecision.

After an epic struggle, Mama extracted herself and lumbered to the car, wearing a noxious black substance that was already hardening into a white crust. After a long, smelly and very silent ride, we stopped at a gas station, where the attendant hosed Mama off, snickering the whole time.

Ellen Evans Whiting Princeton, NJ

TWIN TROUBLE

She understood it took patience to deal with her and her sister.

In the '40s, coming from a family of 12, my twin sister, Lois, and I had little money for entertainment. My Uncle Harry and Aunt Gracie came to our rescue and took us with them on a road trip. Lois and I were known for talking constantly and giggling a lot—our family called it "twin talk" that only the two of us could understand. We hadn't traveled far when the twin talk started. Uncle Harry quickly lost his patience. He told us that if we didn't stop talking, he was going to put us out of the car and make us walk. We tried so hard to be quiet, but soon we were talking and giggling again. Uncle Harry stopped the car and told us to get out! We were shocked but slowly got out of the car and watched while Uncle Harry drove off, leaving us on a very lonely road.

He and Aunt Gracie went only around the next bend; then they stopped and peeked around to check on us. We looked so lost and helpless…and quiet. So he drove back! Of course, Lois and I started up again, but they must have learned to live with it.

The first night, we stopped at a place that had individual cabins; Lois and I had our own and fell asleep immediately. When we woke up, we could see the sun rising. We hurried to get up and dressed and presented ourselves at our uncle's cabin door, thinking he would be so proud of us. He came to the door yawning and looked surprised. We told him we were ready to go! He looked at his watch and told us we had been asleep only an hour, and the sun was going down, not coming up!

The next evening, we headed home. Lois and I accepted my aunt's offer of a Coke (yum!). But after we arrived home, Uncle Harry opened the back door to find two girls fast asleep and Coke all over the floor!

Even after that, my generous aunt and uncle continued to include our siblings and us in their adventures. When we get bogged down with everyday worries, we stop to remember those good times we had and the good people in our lives.
Louise Pierce Tremont, MS

Lois and Louise have enjoyed "twin talk" and giggling through the years.

Motorcycle Man

Dad lived his life on a Harley-Davidson and took his family along for the ride.

I remember the happiness I felt as I waited in front of my school and heard the sound of Dad's Harley-Davidson motorcycle. My father, William Whipp, usually came to pick me up from school, which was about a mile from our home in Springfield, Ohio. I'd hop in the sidecar and away we'd go.

Dad, who was born in 1876, never owned a car. He started out with a "penny-farthing" bicycle that had one big wheel and one small one, progressed to regular bicycles and then to motorcycles. Back in 1934, the year I was born, someone gave him a car, but he sold it.

"Motorcycles were still in style," explained Dad, who believed that cycles were safer than cars.

Dad lived his life on Harleys and brought my mother, Eva, and me along for the ride. Mom and I took turns riding behind him on the double seat or next to him in the sidecar, the kind you might see in old films.

The three of us often took short trips together. In the summers, we'd pack up the Harley and head north to visit cousins who lived on Higgins Lake in Michigan. In 1946, Dad got a deal on a new model, and my parents decided we'd go to Snoqualmie Falls, Washington, to visit one of Dad's brothers. For the 5,375-mile round trip, Mom and Dad packed the sidecar compartment and the saddlebags with a small tent, a kerosene cooking unit, food and extra clothes, and away we went.

There weren't many motels back then, but it didn't matter because we couldn't afford to stay in one. When it started getting dark, Dad would look for a farm with a big yard, then stop and ask the owner if we could set up the tent for the night.

We bought fresh food along the way and used the restrooms of gas stations (which were usually outhouses) for the purpose of cleaning up daily. I recall getting such a bad sun- and windburn on my nose that it peeled for several years afterward.

I was in awe of the vast expanse of our country. When we had a hard time going up the Rockies, Dad was concerned that the cycle was losing power. He didn't know what the Continental Divide was or why the Harley barely moved up those mountains even though he was accelerating. Finally someone in a repair shop explained what was happening.

My memories of the great West include the geysers in Yellowstone National Park, particularly Old Faithful; the petrified trees there; and the big animals, especially bison, deer and bears. Everything was so large in this fascinating world!

Finally we reached Washington and connected with our relatives. My father's brother had five children, one of whom had two daughters close to my age. I had a great time wading in the Pacific Ocean with them.

When it was time to head home we took a southern route. Stopping at the Great Salt Lake in Utah was the first adventure on the return trip. I had a hard time really believing that one could float on it; I didn't try it.

Then we crossed into the northern deserts of Arizona and New Mexico and discovered totally different landscapes. I think we probably took the famed Route 66.

When we got home Dad made a big discovery: He found his driver's license in an old billfold. He hadn't been carrying it on our trip. Luckily we made that entire journey without ever being stopped by the police, except to look us over and ask Dad how he could make such a trip on a motorcycle with his family!

I felt very worldly and grown-up as I told stories of our trip to my friends back home. I've lived in California since 1964 and made many trips to Ohio and back, but never again did I experience the wonder and diversity of the U.S. as I did when I was 12.

Mabel (seated) saw the wonders of the West with her parents, William and Eva.

Mabel Marie Whipp Dameron San Francisco, CA

Below: We had traveled 60 miles on a gallon of gas each. Here Betty and Baby relax during lunch at an abandoned house near Meridian, Mississippi.

Above: Larry in Americus, Georgia, on day eight of the trip. It was so windy and cold, we made camp early. He bought a frozen chicken, potatoes and cheese, and we had a wonderful meal that night.

CROSS-COUNTRY MOTOR SCOOTER ADVENTURE

Speed was not the objective for this couple's travels.

My husband, Larry, and I kept a diary of our 1953 trip across the United States, from east to west and south to north. Starting in Richmond, Virginia, where we bought two Allstate motor scooters, we spent more than 65 days on the road, camping, sleeping in cabins or staying with friends. We could travel a maximum speed of only 44 mph, but we were able to get up to 118 miles per gallon of gas. Our cat, Baby, made the trip with us too!

Betty Mertsching

VIP at the 1939-40 New York World's Fair

Midwestern girl experiences more than she could dream when she wins a trip.

A s an 11-year-old farm girl, I won the trip of a lifetime: an all-expenses-paid family vacation to the New York World's Fair. It was part of a national contest in which newspapers worked with fair officials to select one "typical American family" from each state. We represented Minnesota, and I'll never forget our 17-day adventure.

On the morning of May 29, 1940, a chauffeur arrived at our farmhouse in a shiny new Ford. On the five-day trip to New York City, we went sightseeing and stayed at only the best hotels.

When we finally arrived at the fair, Harvey Gibson, chairman of the fair board, escorted us to the house where we would live for a week. We had our own maid to prepare our meals, wash and iron our clothes, and keep the house tidy. I'd never known luxury like this before!

I still remember the first time I saw the towering Trylon and giant Perisphere, both located in the center of the fairgrounds. These structures fit the fair's "World of Tomorrow" theme and attracted a steady stream of spectators. You could go inside the Perisphere and stand on a moving sidewalk to view a futuristic metropolis called Democracity.

My family followed a daily itinerary to see the many exhibitions. As VIPs, we got to cut into long lines as we entered exhibits.

In pavilions, companies predicted the future technologies for day-to-day life. I loved the General Electric building and its House of Magic, full of appliances for the home. It seemed wondrous to our family, because our farm had no running water and wouldn't have electricity until that

The Petersens marvel at their first sight of the fair in 1940.

summer! I couldn't wait to experience these modern conveniences.

We also got a glimpse of cultures from around the world. Geography and history were suddenly more interesting to this schoolgirl.

During our free time, we used our passes for all the midway rides. The roller coaster was a thrill! In the evening, we saw entertaining shows and watched spectacular fireworks.

When our week at the fair ended, each of us children received a gift. My brother, Alfred Jr., got a baseball signed by Babe Ruth, while I got a bracelet with Trylon and Perisphere charms.

Can you imagine what this trip meant to a girl from the Midwest who attended a one-room school? It started my lifelong interest in travel and education. Though it's been decades since our trip, I can still picture the New York World's Fair in all its glory.

Joyce Petersen Youngren Mesa, AZ

I still remember the first time I saw the towering Trylon and giant Perisphere...

TESTOSTERONE MEETS T. REX

Spending the day with family and prehistoric creatures.

Many of the exhibits at the 1964-'65 World's Fair in Queens, New York, gave attendees a glimpse into the future. However, one exhibit took spectators into the distant past. Dinoland, sponsored by Sinclair Oil Corp., featured life-size replicas of nine dinosaurs, including Dino, a 70-foot-long version of Sinclair's signature Brontosaurus, plus there was a Tyrannosaurus rex and a triceratops.

A year after the fair closed, Dinoland embarked on a multicity tour, stopping at the Northland Mall in Columbus, Ohio, 30 miles from my hometown of Stoutsville. My three brothers and I just had to see it.

John Scanlan Hilton Head Island, SC

John's mom, Dorothy, kept an eye on baby Kathy while the boys (from left, John, Jeff, Joe and Jerry) spent the day teaching their dad all about dinosaurs.

Taking it to New York

In 1964 my Aunt Sybil, who served on the Alabama Public Service Commission, got an invitation to the New York World's Fair. She asked me, my mom and my sister Lynn to join her. We left Birmingham, stayed at the New York Hilton, ate at the Four Seasons and saw a Broadway play. Oh, and the fair was great, too. It was the trip of a lifetime.

Benjamin Pool Montgomery, AL

Little Bear or Big Bear?

Vacationers are taken by surprise at Yellowstone.

My family took a road trip out West in 1936, and one of our stops was Yellowstone National Park. When we pulled up to Old Faithful Inn, Mother pointed out a crowd of people gathered at a railing some distance away. We could see them in a meadow opposite the hotel.

She checked her watch. "It's nearly time. Just keep looking in that direction."

I stared over at the crowd. Suddenly, steam shot up out of the ground. I heard a loud roar as water hurtled skyward, and I ducked away fast, aiming for Mother's arms. She said, "Don't be scared, honey; that's just Old Faithful. It's a geyser that goes off like that every hour, and it's never been known to miss a time. That's why they call it Old Faithful."

We were staying in Cabin 19 at the far end of a long row of rough-hewn log structures. As we walked on the path toward the cabin, we saw a bear cub strolling along by itself. Daddy chuckled. We moved faster than the cub, so it was soon behind us. Then we passed a family around a card table in the middle of the path. The table was loaded with food, and everyone seemed jolly. Finally, we arrived at Cabin 19; there was a kerosene lantern on the table, since there was no electricity.

Then I heard a commotion outside. We stepped to the doorway and saw our neighbors emerging from their cabins. Someone pointed over to the next section and hollered, "Bear!"

There was yelling and a crash, and the picnickers came running. "There's a big bear!" screamed one lady. "Help! Get a ranger!"

We heard that the card table had collapsed, and in the middle of the mess sat the cub, contentedly munching. Next to it sprawled a huge brown bear, also feasting on the snacks. Daddy said he felt dumb for not sounding the alarm when we first spotted the cub!

Excerpted from the author's memoir, "Remembery."

Lee Blattner Etiwanda, CA

GRATEFUL FOR A GRAND JOURNEY

Two adults and seven kids travel 11,000 miles in 40 days.

On July 11, 1966, at 11 a.m., my family took off from Vernon, New York, in our 1963 Dodge motor home camper. Leaving the family dairy farm in the hands of relatives, we headed west for an 11,000-mile-long, 40-day trip. To me, this was miraculous! My courageous, adventurous and faith-filled parents survived 40 days with seven children between ages 3 and 17.

We first drove to Battle Creek in Michigan, then to the Kellogg's cereal plant in Iowa, and then to General Grant's home in Illinois. After crossing into South Dakota, we stopped at the Corn Palace, experienced Badlands National Park, saw Mount Rushmore National Memorial, visited Yellowstone National Park (just in time to see Old Faithful erupt), and took a swim in Yellowstone Lake. I remember seeing moose and a bear get a bit too close to my dad, who was outside filming.

Next, we went to Montana's Glacier National Park and had a brief snowball fight near the Hungry Horse Dam. Eventually, we arrived in California, where we saw the famous redwood trees and drove over the Golden Gate Bridge. We also camped on a beach along the Pacific coast, touched the handprints in cement along the Hollywood Walk of Fame and, of course, experienced every child's dream: Disneyland.

Next, we took a swim in Lake Mead in Nevada and saw the Hoover Dam. In Arizona, we stopped to see the Grand Canyon, and then we made our way up to Utah to see Bryce Canyon and the Great Salt Lake. Our last memorable stop: an overnight stay in Niagara Falls.

The trip came full circle as we arrived home in Vernon, New York, at 5:30 p.m., just in time for supper.

Denise Dee Kitchen Clinton, NY

My family standing in front of the 1963 Dodge motor home we drove on our cross-country trek.

ISLAND PARADISE

Coming back to the same special place year after year brings joy.

For some 20 years beginning in the '60s, our family spent the last week of July at North Beach Inn on Orcas Island in the San Juan archipelago of the Pacific Northwest. Usually about eight or 10 of us were able to get away for that special time. We always reserved our favorite cabins, Sleepy Hollow and Night Owl, which are side by side on the beach.

We would drive to Anacortes, Washington, where we boarded the ferry and anticipated the week ahead as we passed many small islands along the way.

Finally, we'd arrive at North Beach. The first thing we did was blow up our rubber dinghy with a foot pump. Then my niece would load the crab pots with raw chicken pieces as bait and set them out, hoping to catch enough fresh crab for dinner that evening. The rest of us would unload the cars and set things up in the cabins.

Next, we'd walk down to the beach, where we would pick up shells and look for agates. Some of us just sat there enjoying the scenery until it was time to fix dinner.

On one trip, I was in the cabin when my niece came running, yelling, "Come see the whales!" We ran out to see a group of orcas cavorting, jumping and slapping their flukes not far from shore. We watched in amazement. It seemed that they were putting on a show just for us.

When the week was over and we turned in our keys at the front office, we were sure to make our reservations for the following year.
June K. Winter Shoreline, WA

The beach on the north side of Orcas Island was the spot for floating on a rubber dinghy. Dogs joined the family (above) in making memories on the island.

Sitting on the fender of the family's 1927 Willys-Knight, Ernie posed with his father and mother, Ernest and Clara, and sister Ruthellen in 1936 after driving through the Wawona Tree in Yosemite National Park.

THE STEEP AND WINDING ROAD

Driving there took a lot longer in the 1930s.

My family spent many vacations in Sequoia and Yosemite national parks in the 1930s. Sequoia was my favorite because it had the General Sherman Tree, the largest tree by volume in the world.

Sequoia also had Moro Rock, which was scary to climb even though the steps were carved into the rock and there were steel-cable handrails to hold. Big brown bears also raided the trash cans outside the cabins at night. We would visit the garbage dump just to watch the bears scavenge for food.

We lived in Los Angeles and traveled over the Ridge Route, on Highway 99, to Bakersfield, where we'd stay overnight in a motor court; it took more than a day to get to Sequoia back then. The Ridge Route was a steep and winding two-lane road, and we had to carry canvas water bags and stop to get water for the radiator.

Ernie Ogren Torrance, CA

Decisions Made Easy

Dressing alike was just one way this family enjoyed vacation fun.

After six children, my husband, Jack, and I decided camping would be a good thing for the whole family. And so we jumped in with both feet and bought a tent trailer.

Most of the camper units we found in the 1960s were designed with pop-up tents that pulled out from both sides of the trailer to form the bed areas. Ours was a bit different. The tent pulled out from just one side of the trailer and we staked it to the ground.

Jack and I slept on an air mattress in the trailer bed, while the children sacked out on the floor of the tent in their sleeping bags.

With all of us wearing matching clothes, it was fairly easy to keep track of everyone.

Jack and JoAnn, far left, headed west in 1965 with six kids. After two more, the couple sold their pop-up camper, bottom left, and rented a motor home in 1971, near left. Below, Connie, Pat, Mary and Mike in Nevada in 1966.

Before heading out on our first excursion, Jack bought hardboard and designed and built travel boxes for our belongings: four two-part boxes for our clothing and two cabinets with drawers for pots and pans, kitchen utensils, dishes, cups and flatware. These two cabinets stacked to create a stand for our camping stove. When packed just right, the boxes fit snugly into the storage area under the trailer with little room to spare.

Meanwhile, I planned our camping wardrobes. We wore blue jeans and matching blue- or red-checked or plain blue shirts. With all of us wearing matching clothes, it was fairly easy to keep track of everyone. For Mass on Sundays, I made denim skirts so the girls and I didn't have to wear jeans.

We were very organized as we hit the road to campgrounds in and around Southern California. Then one summer we set out even further and visited relatives in Ohio.

Each night before we went to sleep, we lined up everyone's shoes on a rug outside the tent's screen door. One memorable night, somewhere in Kansas or Missouri, a sudden rain shower hit.

We didn't have this kind of surprise when we were in California. Boy, did we scramble to grab the shoes and drag them into the tent before they got wet!

That camping setup served us for quite a few years. But by the time we had two more children, our traveling arrangements needed upgrading. We rented a motor home for a five-week road trip across the U.S. It still required organization, but was easier and more comfortable than setting up and taking down a tent every night. Only one drawback—it wasn't really camping anymore.

JoAnn Schueller Cooke Prescott, AZ

THE LITTLE GREEN TENT

Close quarters didn't prevent this family from making happy memories.

In the early '60s, an aunt and uncle gave us a tiny green tent. Outside of the Girl Scouts, I had no camping experience, but that didn't stop my family.

Our first trip was to Sylvan Lake in the Black Hills with our two oldest boys.

Next we camped in Mackinac Island State Park, with two more of our boys. From our campsite, we could see the great bridge! Another year took us to Mammoth Cave and Cumberland Falls in Kentucky.

Our last trip was to Rocky Mountain National Park in Colorado. All six of us slept in that little tent (that helped keep us warm some nights)! We roughed it without a stove, using a grill set on empty soda cans over the campfire. We never had a cooler, so we ate a lot of canned chicken and noodles, Dinty Moore stew, and canned spaghetti. My boys still tell me how much they hated powdered milk!

That tent was even set up in our backyard so the boys could sleep out with their friends. It just had to be moved every few days so it wouldn't ruin the grass.

Decades later, the kids still talk about the good times we had with that little green tent.
Ann Hoffmann Hale West Bend, WI

We ate a lot of Dinty Moore stew and canned spaghetti when camping.

Stylish Anglers

My husband, Bob (on left), his nephew Dennis McClanahan and Dennis' dad, Dave, caught these fish on a trip in the Colorado Rockies. I like to think their different hats gave them good luck.
Marlene Barnes Tulsa, OK

Cabin Summers

My kids Beverly, Kevin and Patricia—along with Simon the cat—have a snack on the wagon (below) at the family's lakefront cabin in 1958. We moved to the lake the day school was out and didn't move home until school started in fall. When we got there, it was like turning horses out to pasture. No lessons—only play.
Gertrude Woehrlin Spokane Valley, WA

Something Fishy

As Dad (above at right) bent over to start our outboard motor one day in 1956, this little tarpon jumped into our boat and smacked his back. At first Dad thought I was hitting him with an oar!
David Aldridge Jr. New Hope, AL

CAMPFIRES AND BEAR SCARES

Roughing it when camping is really what makes it exciting.

When I was growing up in the '40s and '50s, my family did not have a lot of money. Instead of going camping, we and all of our neighbors would get together to plan a camp-out in our backyards. At that time, there were no fences and all the yards ran into one another.

We would put out cots, small tents and sleeping bags. At night we would barbecue and eat in camp chairs. It was exciting to stay outside all night and look at the stars. In those days, you knew all of your neighbors within a four-block radius.

Linda Quinlivan Facebook

My family used to camp in Granite Basin in California. It was quite a deserted place. One morning, I was a bit bored while waiting for everyone to wake up and decided to go outside to play. I somehow got it into my head that it would be fun to make some animal tracks in the dirt. Mind you, I was so young that I didn't have a clue as to how the tracks should look.

When my dad got up to make coffee, he noticed the tracks and freaked out. Apparently I had made some pretty convincing bear tracks. He ran to get a gun and told everyone to stay inside. I quietly mentioned that

I had made the tracks. I got into trouble for being a goof-off, but nowadays, I laugh about it.

Wendy Smith Facebook

A favorite place to camp was in New Hampshire. One time, my family was going from our neighbor's camper to ours in the dark. Our toy poodle brushed my dad on the leg, and he thought it was the local bear, Matilda. He yelled for my mom to help him, as though she could fight off a bear. We have been teasing him about it for years.

Denise Datu Facebook

TIME FOR SOME R&R

Everyone needs a vacation once in a while to recharge, so pack up and bring the kids along.

1949

PHOTO-OP

After WWII, families were all smiles again as they took to the road for summer getaways. In a nod to shifting roles, many Kodak ads, including this one from *Look*, had women snapping the shots.

1960

TAKING A HOLIDAY

Whether traveling to the beach, mountains or desert, plan ahead and stay in touch while you are away using Bell Telephone System, as this colorful ad suggests. In the '60s, making arrangements for a trip and being away from one's everyday life took a lot more planning.

HAPPY CAMPERS

The Thompson family enjoys the great outdoors.

1. It takes a few tables to seat all the kids at a picnic party in 1964. The four Thompson children are among the hungry throng.

2. Steve, 11, and sister Ann, 9, check on the fish in August 1963.

3. A 1962 bird's-eye view of the camp shows towels drying after a recent swim.

4. A seasoned camper since the '50s, dad, Bruce, was a packing expert by July 1960.

5. Mom, Joyce, washes dishes in July 1963. She had a pact with Bruce that he would do all the cooking on their camping trips.

Joyce Thompson
Waukesha, WI

We enjoyed it when he brought a fresh salmon back to camp and Mom would fry it up for supper.

At left, Gloria's dad fishes with her mom's sisters; above, Gloria and Donald in 1950.

Those Were the Days

Camping out in a homemade tent was the best!

My fondest childhood summer memories are of our family camping trips to Point Leamington, Newfoundland. We began those two-week summer holiday trips in 1947 when I was just 6 years old, and they continued until I was 14.

My parents, two older sisters Marilyn and Ruth, our younger brother Donald and I would travel from Botwood to Leamington in the back of a hired truck over a gravel road, with all the necessary equipment, including a tent my mother made from cotton flour sacks. She'd bleach them to remove the printing, then sew them together. Dad coated it with some sort of oil to make it waterproof. We had no refrigeration, so Mom canned and bottled food, and brought some store-bought canned food.

Our parents had made friends with Chesley Boone and his family, who lived in Leamington. He was kind enough to let our family set up our tent in their fenced garden every year.

We kids made our own fun playing board games and swimming during the day, while most evenings we'd walk the half-hour each way to a small variety store to buy treats.

We all loved Leamington—especially Dad, who was an avid salmon fisherman. He spent most of his days fishing by the nearby falls. We enjoyed it when he brought a fresh salmon back to camp and Mom would fry it up for supper. What great memories I have of those bygone summers!

Gloria Young Botwood, NL

SIZE SMALL

My brother Jeff (right) and I proudly hold up our first-ever fishing catch in 1959.
We're at the back of the family's 1957 Ford station wagon at Ohio's Lake Logan,
about 40 minutes southeast of Columbus.

Greg Groom Columbus, OH

AROUND THE TABLE

Delicious food and time with family go hand in hand, and the recipes shared through the years easily become treasures with staying power.

BAKING WITH THE DOUGHBOY

Making more than recipes in the kitchen.

I have many memories of my mom's Pillsbury recipes and treasured cookbooks that she saved for more than 40 years (below).

Both my mom and her mother were excellent cooks and bakers, and some of my happiest memories are of my mom teaching me how to bake.

My mother loved trying new recipes. She would send away for a free recipe booklet whenever she saw a coupon for one on the back of a package. When I was a kid, we used to have Pillsbury crescent rolls or biscuits for special dinners, and I'm guessing her collection of Pillsbury Bake-Off cookbooks came from her clipping those proofs of purchase.

Now that I'm a mom myself, I am eager to revisit some of these classics with my own daughters.
Diane Frieden Forest Hills, NY

A selection of Diane's 1970s and 1980s Pillsbury cookbooks from her mom.

Pillsbury Bake-Off contestants often used the company's quick-bake products in winning recipes, such as in Pepperoni 'n' Cheese Crescents (top center).

Snacks

PEPPERONI 'N' CHEESE CRESCENTS

PREPARATION TIME
NUMBER OF SERVINGS
SOURCE OF RECIPE

D
I
S
H

2 cans (8 oz. each) Pillsbury refrigerated

crescent dinner rolls

24 slices pepperoni (1½ in. diameter)

2 slices provolone or low-moisture part-skim

mozzarella cheese (4 in. diameter), quartered

1 egg white, slightly beaten

1. Heat oven to 375°. Separate dough into 8 triangles.

2. Place 3 slices of pepperoni, slightly overlapping, on center of each triangle; top pepperoni with cheese

quarter. Roll up, starting at shortest side of triangle and moving to opposite point.

3. Place rolls seam side down on ungreased cookie sheet; curve into crescent shape. Brush rolls with egg

white. Bake 10 to 14 minutes or until golden brown.

REFILL NO. 801 R

PRIZED SOUTHERN BELLES

Bond grew through baking with one another.

Gertie Johnson (left); Nancy still has Gertie's original recipe card (below) with all the grease stains a beloved dish accumulates.

My grandmother Gertie Johnson had a reputation for being a wonderful cook and baker. During World War II, Gertie baked my father's favorite cookies—Southern Belles—and mailed them to him while he was away in the Army. She wrote to him faithfully every day for two years, and he kept all her letters in a shoebox.

After the war, my father and mother married. My mother said that she always looked forward to going to her mother-in-law's house for Sunday dinners and that she and Gertie became "baking buddies." Gertie gave my mother her prized recipe for Southern Belles, and the cookies have been in our family ever since.

Nancy Krampert Selinsgrove, PA

DISH

SOUTHERN BELLES

PREPARATION TIME
NUMBER OF SERVINGS
SOURCE OF RECIPE

		Meringue Topping:
2 tbsp. butter	1 tsp. baking powder	
1 cup sugar	½ tsp. salt	1 egg white, beaten
2 eggs (save 1 egg white for meringue topping)	2 tbsp. milk	1 cup brown sugar
	½ tsp. lemon juice	½ tsp. vanilla
1½ cups flour	½ tsp. vanilla	⅔ cup shredded coconut

1. Preheat oven to 325°. Blend butter and sugar together in a medium-sized bowl and then add eggs. Sift flour, baking powder and salt, and add them to the butter mixture along with the milk. Add lemon juice and vanilla. Mix well and spread the mixture ¼ in. thick in a shallow greased pan.

2. Make the meringue topping by beating egg white, brown sugar, vanilla and coconut until stiff.

3. Spread the meringue on top of the dough and bake at 325°. Cut into squares and cool before removing from the pan.

STYLECRAFT, BALTO. 30, MD.   PRINTED IN U.S.A.

REFILL NO. 801 R

SUGAR COOKIES

PREPARATION TIME
NUMBER OF SERVINGS
SOURCE OF RECIPE

Cookies:	1 cup buttermilk	Icing:
2 cups sugar	4 cups flour	½ lb. powdered sugar
1 cup lard or Crisco	2 tsp. baking powder	½ stick of butter
2 eggs	½ tsp. salt	Vanilla
1 tsp. baking soda	1 tsp. vanilla	A little milk

Preheat oven to 400°. Cream sugar and lard; add 2 eggs and beat again. Stir baking soda into buttermilk; let sit for 5 minutes, then mix with creamed sugar and lard. Add 2 cups flour, baking powder, salt and vanilla; beat until mixed, then add remaining flour. Mix well but briefly. Pat out with hands to about ¼ in. thick on floured cutting board, then cut with floured cutter. Bake 7 to 9 minutes on greased baking sheet until edges are brown and tops are nearly brown. For icing, mix powdered sugar, butter and vanilla while adding just enough milk to make smooth. Makes 30 big heart-shaped cookies or about 40 round cookies.

STYLECRAFT, BALTO. 30, MD.   PRINTED IN U.S.A.

REFILL NO. 801 R

GRANDMA NEIFERD'S COUNTY FAIR-WINNING COOKIES

There was a secret to the softness in these special sugary treats.

My grandmother Mary Katherine Neiferd was raised in the central part of Ohio, where many German immigrants settled. In fact, while she was growing up, her household spoke mostly German. This recipe is for her soft sugar cookies—the secret to the softness is real lard and whole buttermilk.

The cookies were very popular at the church bazaar. Back in the 1950s and 1960s, before there were plastic containers for food storage, she would carry the cookies in big, wide dress boxes she got from a shop downtown. She sold her cookies to restaurants in Lima, Ohio, where Grandpa Neiferd worked at the Lima Locomotive Works.

After she passed, I was the only one with the patience and knack to make her cookies. Before I moved away, some of the older church ladies who had memories of the bazaars would beg me to bring them some cookies whenever I baked them.

Now, for Valentine's Day, I make big, soft heart cookies with pink icing and mail them to relatives across the country. I serve them with icing, but Grandma usually just sprinkled sugar or a few raisins on top. I even won a blue ribbon for best sugar cookie at the local county fair with the recipe.

Whenever I make these cookies, I think of Grandma watching over me and hope I am making her proud.
Candy Neiferd Davis Florence, SC

BANANA-NUT OR PLUM?

Cakes are sweet, but the ones passed down through generations are sweeter.

BANANA-NUT CAKE

DISH

PREPARATION TIME
NUMBER OF SERVINGS
SOURCE OF RECIPE

3 large (or 4 medium) extra-ripe bananas, sliced

1½ cups sugar

2 eggs

1 cup oil

½ tsp. salt

1 tsp. baking soda

2 cups flour

1 cup walnuts, chopped finely

Put bananas in one bowl; sprinkle with baking soda. In a second bowl, mix sugar, eggs, flour, oil and salt.

Add banana and baking soda mixture; blend. Add walnuts; mix well. Pour into 13x9-in. greased pan;

do not flour pan. Bake at 325° or 350° for about 30 minutes. Do not frost.

PLUM CAKE

DISH

PREPARATION TIME
NUMBER OF SERVINGS
SOURCE OF RECIPE

1¼ cups sifted flour

1½ tsp. baking powder

½ tsp. salt

¼ cup sugar

¼ cup shortening

1 egg

¼ cup milk

½ tsp. lemon extract

22 plums (for best results, use small Italian plums)

5 tbsp. margarine

¼ cup packed light brown sugar

Cinnamon

Sift together 1 cup flour, baking powder, salt and sugar. Blend in shortening. Beat egg with milk and lemon extract; add to mixture. Spread batter in a very thin layer in greased and floured 12x9-in. pan. Halve plums lengthwise and remove pits; place halves, skin side down, on dough. For crumb mixture on top of fruit, mix 2 tbsp. margarine, remaining ¼ cup flour and light brown sugar. Bake at 400° for 25 minutes, then pour 3 tbsp. melted margarine on top and sprinkle with cinnamon. Bake 10 more minutes.

STYLECRAFT. BALTO. 30, MD.   PRINTED IN U.S.A.

. REFILL NO. 801 R

Cherished Recipe

This banana-nut cake recipe has been in my family for more than 50 years. Now my teenage great-grandson carries on the tradition.
Sarah Shipley Highland, CA

Fall Dessert

I saved my mother's treasured plum cake recipe. I like to make the tart treat for my daughter's October birthday—perfectly timed to plum season!
Irene Lang Farmington Hills, MI

COOKIES WORTH CRAVING

One never tires of delicious goodies.

DISH	NO-BAKE COOKIES	PREPARATION TIME
		NUMBER OF SERVINGS
		SOURCE OF RECIPE

2 cups sugar	¼ tsp. salt
½ cup milk	3 cups quick oats
½ cup shortening	½ cup peanut butter
4 tbsp. cocoa	1 tsp. vanilla

Boil sugar, milk, shortening, cocoa and salt for 1 minute; mix in oats, peanut butter and vanilla. Drop by spoonfuls onto waxed paper. (Give to William.)

STYLECRAFT, BALTO. 30. MD.   PRINTED IN U.S.A.

REFILL NO. 801 R

My mother, Ilah Mae Horton, would often make cookies, and my favorites were her no-bake chocolate peanut butter oatmeal cookies. She had received the recipe from a friend in Milwaukee. I could not get enough—I'd eat them hot right off the spoon, cold from the freezer or at room temperature off the counter.

One time Mom decided to see if she could make me sick of them. She whipped up batch after batch after batch, but I didn't get tired of eating them before she got tired of making them.

I'd receive them once in a while as a gift to share with the family, but when I'd get home, I would quietly hide them and hog them all. Sure, the others resented that, but I didn't care!

William L. Horton Forsyth, IL

BREAKFAST OF CHAMPIONS

Grandmas sure know how to spoil the little ones.

TV dinners hadn't been on the market long when I got my first taste of the forbidden fare in the early 1960s. My mother wouldn't let us have them at home. But when my brother Bill and I went to visit my grandparents in Abilene, Texas, we saw our chance.

Bill and I loved Mexican food, so he asked our Grandmother McCormick to buy us enchilada TV dinners as a treat. The next morning, I found Bill in the kitchen eating one. And to my delight, there was one for me, too, along with a Dr Pepper and a chocolate-covered ice cream bar. What a wonderful breakfast we had!

She thought she was spoiling her youngest grandchildren, but I also suspect she was secretly proud of her rebellion against the typical healthy breakfast.

Paula McCormick Cawthon Denison, TX

COOL FOR THE KITCHEN

Sleek tableware for midcentury modern families.

1955

CLEAR WINNER

To celebrate its 50th anniversary in 1955, Anchor Hocking created Golden Anniversary dinnerware in the Swirl pattern trimmed in 22K gold (top, foreground). Today's collectors love Anchor Hocking's sturdy Fire-King and Jade-ite glassware.

1955

GOURMET SELECTION

Homer Laughlin's curvy Epicure line debuted in 1955. Created by the company's design director Don Schreckengost, Epicure was similar to Russel Wright's china from rival Steubenville Pottery. But Epicure didn't sell well and was discontinued.

1954

SHAPED FOR SUCCESS

Gladding, McBean & Co.'s reputation for innovation grew after Mary Grant, former art director at Macy's, joined. Her Encanto line was selected for the Museum of Modern Art's "Good Design" exhibit. The ad at far right shows Encanto in an array of pearly colors—an elegant answer to the bold hues of Homer Laughlin's Fiesta line.

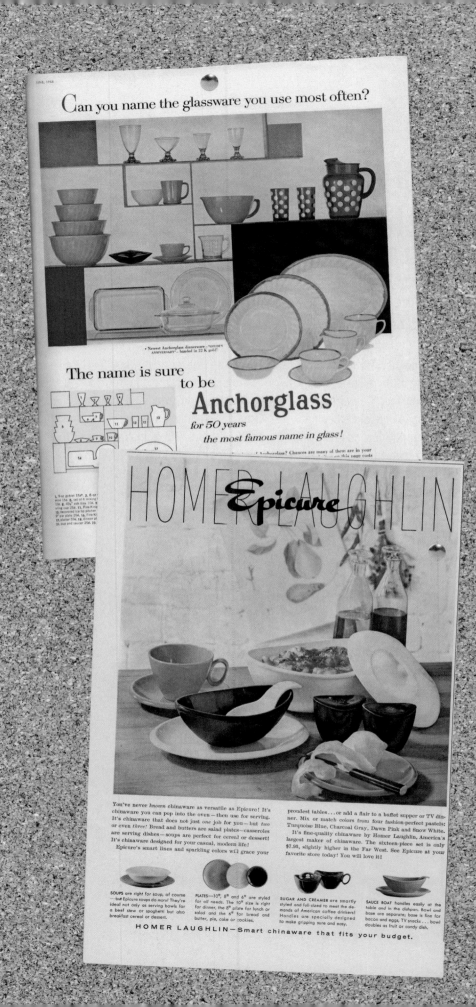

Can you name the glassware you use most often?

• Newest Anchorglass dinnerware—"GOLDEN ANNIVERSARY"—banded in 22 K gold!

The name is sure to be **Anchorglass** for 50 years the most famous name in glass!

HOMER LAUGHLIN *Epicure*

You've never *known* chinaware as versatile as Epicure! It's chinaware you can pop into the oven—then use for serving. It's chinaware that does not just *one* job for you—but *two* or even *three!* Bread and butters are salad plates—casseroles are serving dishes—soups are perfect for cereal or dessert! It's chinaware designed for your casual, modern life! Epicure's smart lines and sparkling colors will grace your proudest tables...or add a flair to a buffet supper or TV dinner. Mix or match colors from four fashion-perfect pastels: Turquoise Blue, Charcoal Gray, Dawn Pink and Snow White. It's fine-quality chinaware by Homer Laughlin, America's largest maker of chinaware. The sixteen-piece set is only $7.95, slightly higher in the Far West. See Epicure at your favorite store today! You will love it!

SOUPS are right for soup, of course—but Epicure soups do more! They're ideal not only as serving bowls for a beef stew or spaghetti but also breakfast cereal or dessert.

PLATES—10", 8" and 6" are styled for all needs. The 10" size is right for dinner, the 8" plate for lunch or salad and the 6" for bread and butter, pie, cake or cookies.

SUGAR AND CREAMER are smartly styled and full-sized to meet the demands of American coffee drinkers! Handles are specially designed to make gripping sure and easy.

SAUCE BOAT handles easily at the table and in the dishpan. Bowl and base are separate; base is fine for bacon and eggs, TV snacks...bowl doubles as fruit or candy dish.

HOMER LAUGHLIN—Smart chinaware that fits your budget.

All from Memory

Three generations later, these delicacies are still made.

When my grandmother came to America from Italy, she brought with her the recipe for scrupelle, a fried-dough dessert. The holiday season always calls for a special recipe, and Grandma insisted this delicacy be made fresh on Christmas Eve, as was the custom in the old country. Before Grandpa even cared to make an appearance, Grandma had mixed the dough.

She began her process by taking out a mixing bowl, a breadboard bigger than any you'd see today and a huge white cloth—all of which had come with her from Italy. She placed ingredients on the table: bread flour, a large yeast cake, a dish of lard, three eggs, salt, sugar and five medium-sized potatoes (to be peeled, boiled and mashed). She used her hands and eyes as measuring tools.

She first prepared the potatoes for cooking and mashing. Then, in a small bowl, she crumbled the cake of yeast and dissolved it in water. She poured a can of evaporated milk, diluted with warm water, into a large bowl and added the dissolved yeast, a few small chunks of softened lard, the eggs (well beaten), and a scant handful of salt and sugar. The mashed potatoes and flour went in last, one spoonful at a time, until the dough was stiff. At that point, Grandma's hands became the mixer.

The dough was put onto the floured breadboard, and Grandma would knead it slowly, adding flour until it was soft. With great ceremony, Grandma wrapped the board—dough and all—with the white cloth and placed it on the stove. She then whispered a blessing in her native language.

About three hours later, the dough would look as if it had doubled in size—just like magic! Then Grandma would bring out a large iron frying pan (still in the family!) and use it to melt a chunk of lard over a flame. To see if the lard was hot enough, she would fry a piece of bread. If it turned golden brown quickly, the lard was ready.

Grandma would dip her hands into the dough, rip off a small piece and stretch it to the size of a pencil. Then she'd gently drop each strip into the hot lard. The dough puffed up like cotton, turning golden brown in just seconds. She placed the strips on brown paper bags (cut out flat) to drain off excess grease. Even though they were hot, no one could resist that first bite.

Joan Doeblin Geneva, NY

> Before Grandpa even cared to make an appearance,
>
> Grandma had mixed the dough.

MAKING MINCEMEAT

A traditional family recipe lives on through granddaughter.

In 1906, my grandma was born on a farm, the second-youngest of eight children. Her family raised or grew everything they ate, and everyone had chores.

When I was young, I always helped my grandma, my mom and two of my grandma's sisters whip up a big batch of mincemeat. Mincemeat is a wonderful pie filling with cooked ground beef, chopped apples and raisins for body, plus spices and other juices for flavor. It took all day to make: We ground the beef very finely with a small hand-crank grinder and cooked it, peeled and chopped nearly a bushel of Jonathan apples, and then mixed and simmered the stuff to perfection.

When the mincemeat was finished, we packed it into glass quart jars and sealed them using a pressure cooker. One quart would make a nice, full pie, and everybody who helped make the mincemeat took home several jars. This all-day project produced anywhere from 20 to 30 jars of mincemeat, and the sealed jars would keep in the basement for years.

I made the mincemeat once as an adult, and it turned out just like Grandma's. I love it!

Every holiday season I think of her because she always had our entire family—20 to 25 people—over to her house to make mincemeat for pies.

She originally wrote the recipe on an envelope, and I love to look at her handwriting and remember her life on the farm. I grew up close to her, and I now live in a new house on the same property. Her house is gone now, but she will always be there.

Connie Hammond Fort Madison, IA

MINCEMEAT

PREPARATION TIME
NUMBER OF SERVINGS
SOURCE OF RECIPE

5 qt. apples, chopped	1 qt. brandy or wine
3 qt. cooked ground beef	1 cup vinegar
3 qt. sugar	1 tbsp. black pepper
2 qt. raisins	1 tbsp. salt
1 qt. suet or butter	2 tsp. cinnamon
1 qt. fruit juice or cider	2 tsp. pumpkin pie spice
1 qt. molasses	Juice of 3 lemons

Put everything into a pot at once. Cook until apples are done.

STYLECRAFT. BALTO. 30, MD.   PRINTED IN U.S.A.

REFILL NO. 801 R

Like Connie, this young girl is learning from her grandma. She is rolling out a pie crust.

ROSELYN'S CHOICE

Grandfather knew what his little granddaughter preferred.

One of my earliest memories is visiting my Italian grandfather's house in Milwaukee's Third Ward. The cobblestone streets were jarring, and the houses, built at the turn of the century or earlier, were so close together that you couldn't see daylight between them. The wind off Lake Michigan, just a few blocks away, was cool in summer, cold in winter.

My *nonno* (Italian for "grandfather") would greet all of his grandchildren by leaning down, pinching our cheeks and giving us a kiss.

His handlebar mustache scratched horribly.

On one of our visits in the summer of 1947, when I was 4, Nonno asked me to join him for breakfast. It was after 1 p.m., and while I felt it was late for breakfast, I was eager to spend time with him. We were going to dine in the family tavern and restaurant downstairs from the living quarters.

He carried me down, stood me up and, while swinging my hand back and forth, asked me in broken English, "Do you a wanna ice cream or do you a wanna pasta?"

I raised my free arm high in the air and answered emphatically, "Pasta!"

Nonno laughed out loud, twirled his mustache, and called to my Uncle Arthur, the youngest of his 10 sons, to come out from the kitchen and take our order.

While we waited for our meal to arrive, Nonno spoke Italian and I spoke English. Somehow, we understood each other. We talked until our food arrived.

Nonno had eggs cooked in tomato sauce, and I had pasta with sauce and meatballs. Yes, pasta! To this day I prefer pasta to ice cream.

Roselyn Stewart Brookfield, WI

Nonno Nunzio Maniaci combs his granddaughter's hair. Uncle Arthur stands outside the family restaurant, the Canadian Club.

Milk. It Does a Body Good.
Sealtest brand milk sponsored this photo taken in 1950 of my family
in our Highland Heights, Kentucky, kitchen. My mom, Loretta, pours
glasses of milk and serves snacks to me and my five brothers (from
left, David, Ralph, Donald holding me on his lap, Charlie and Jimmy).
Jerry Bertram Eau Claire, WI

ROOT BEER WITH GRANDMOTHER

Making this homemade beverage is something she'll never forget.

My grandmother loved root beer. On a hot summer day, while others were gulping down a lemonade, an iced tea or a soda pop, she was loyal to her mug of ice-cold root beer that she'd brewed herself.

I was 5 when I began spending summers with her in Chisholm, Minnesota. I have many memories of sitting on the front-porch swing, looking at the sky flooded with twinkling stars. My favorite memory is from our yearly Fourth of July event. I can still see my grandmother standing at my bedroom door in the morning, saying those magical words: "Wake up, Princess. Time to make our root beer!"

I bolted out of my bed, climbed into my overalls and charged to the cavernous cellar, excited to spend the day making our summer supply of home-brewed root beer! Hours later, exhausted and looking to celebrate a deed well done, we visited the downtown park to watch the glorious fireworks.

I often think of those summer days with my grandmother making old-fashioned root beer!
Lorraine Shank Rocky River, OH

Mom's Pennsylvania Dutch Specialties

Eating heartily was never a problem for this family.

The first doctor my mom had in Florida had lived in Pennsylvania, and when he heard that she was Pennsylvania Dutch, he asked about the foods he remembered. Mom gave him recipes for German apple crisp, copper pennies and apple butter pie.

She used abbreviations to save time—like all great cooks, she knew in her head what she wanted—so some of the inventions and variations that we enjoyed are lost forever.

But cooking any full meal from scratch takes a tremendous amount of work. The Pennsylvania Dutch have sayings on this: *"Wonst net wehrt fir des maul"* ("If it were not for this mouth") and *"De gebrotna dova kumma net ins maul geflowa"* ("The cooked dove won't fly into your mouth"). In other words, if it weren't for our mouths constantly needing food, we would have much more time and energy for other pursuits—or just relaxation.

Sometimes I'd tease Mom when she made a big, delicious meal. "I'll try not to eat much,"

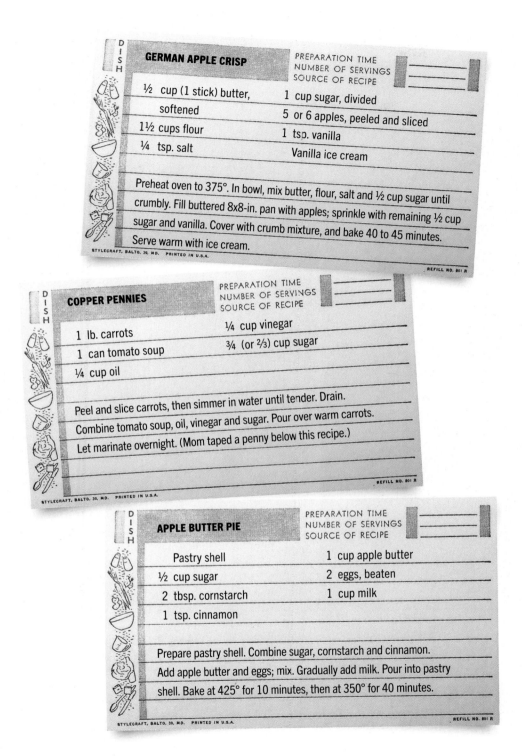

GERMAN APPLE CRISP

PREPARATION TIME
NUMBER OF SERVINGS
SOURCE OF RECIPE

½ cup (1 stick) butter, softened

1½ cups flour

¼ tsp. salt

1 cup sugar, divided

5 or 6 apples, peeled and sliced

1 tsp. vanilla

Vanilla ice cream

Preheat oven to 375°. In bowl, mix butter, flour, salt and ½ cup sugar until crumbly. Fill buttered 8x8-in. pan with apples; sprinkle with remaining ½ cup sugar and vanilla. Cover with crumb mixture, and bake 40 to 45 minutes. Serve warm with ice cream.

STYLECRAFT, BALTO. 30, MD. PRINTED IN U.S.A.   REFILL NO. 801 R

COPPER PENNIES

PREPARATION TIME
NUMBER OF SERVINGS
SOURCE OF RECIPE

1 lb. carrots

1 can tomato soup

¼ cup oil

¼ cup vinegar

¾ (or ⅔) cup sugar

Peel and slice carrots, then simmer in water until tender. Drain.

Combine tomato soup, oil, vinegar and sugar. Pour over warm carrots.

Let marinate overnight. (Mom taped a penny below this recipe.)

STYLECRAFT, BALTO. 30, MD. PRINTED IN U.S.A.   REFILL NO. 801 R

APPLE BUTTER PIE

PREPARATION TIME
NUMBER OF SERVINGS
SOURCE OF RECIPE

Pastry shell

½ cup sugar

2 tbsp. cornstarch

1 tsp. cinnamon

1 cup apple butter

2 eggs, beaten

1 cup milk

Prepare pastry shell. Combine sugar, cornstarch and cinnamon. Add apple butter and eggs; mix. Gradually add milk. Pour into pastry shell. Bake at 425° for 10 minutes, then at 350° for 40 minutes.

STYLECRAFT, BALTO. 30, MD. PRINTED IN U.S.A.   REFILL NO. 801 R

I'd say, "I'll save it for my momma." She'd answer, "Ach, don't talk so dumb! I made it for you to eat."

Then I'd bedevil her a little more and say, "But I don't want to eat my momma out of house and home." Eventually she caught on, and she would pretend to be upset. She'd playfully warn, "Don't you dare…"

So, sweet and obedient kid that I was, I shut up and ate heartily. I'd love to hear once again Mom's delightful call, *"Na cum essa!"* ("Now come eat!")

I know absolutely nothing about cooking, so I hope I copied these recipes correctly!

Ralph C. Smith, Jr. North Charleston, SC

Saving by the Book

Sperry & Hutchinson Green Stamps opened up a catalog of dreams.

Way back around 1976, when I was a young housewife, I learned that my husband loved coleslaw. Eager to please, I'd laboriously grate the cabbage by hand. But sometimes I'd simply cut it in thin slices and try to slip it past him. He knew. He always knew.

As I was also a young mother, I was quite busy; frankly, I had a lot more to do than grate cabbage.

I was faithfully saving Green Stamps at the time—how I saved and saved and saved!—and making frequent visits to the redemption center next to the grocery store in the Comet Plaza in Clarion. I'd wander around inside and think about what I wanted. It wasn't going to be anything frivolous—it had to help me in some way.

And then I saw it: a Hamilton Beach food processor. That thing could buzz through a

Collectors redeemed stamps for goods at dedicated stores or by catalog.

cabbage in no time! Did I have enough stamps? Of course not. It felt like I needed hundreds of books. However, I continued to save, and eventually my patience paid off. For an undetermined (totally forgotten) number of books, I walked out with my cabbage-slicing companion.

It's been decades now and that Hamilton Beach food processor is still working, doing its primary duty of slicing coleslaw for Christmas, New Year's and Easter dinners, Fourth of July cookouts and church potlucks.

I think about the effort I put into saving for this gizmo—how difficult life could be with three children and how this machine made it a bit easier.

I now have seven grandchildren. They don't know the coleslaw on our table has an old story.

Marilyn George Rimersburg, PA

MADE WITH LOVE

It's a common ingredient in these stories.

Mom always let us eat raw cookie dough. One day I begged her for a taste, but it turned out to be shortbread dough—yuck! We were always excited to see rolled and cut cookies because that meant more scraps for us to eat!

Shelley Thompson
Facebook

My mom made fudge quite often. There was no secret recipe—it was right on the back of the cocoa tin. Still, it took patience and a strong arm to get everything just right. Mom had the knack. Just the sight of her pouring the sweet goodness from the pan onto the buttered plate made our mouths water. I have the same recipe, but I don't have the same knack she did!

Margi Dickson Andrulonis
Facebook

One Christmas my grandmother confided in me that she had accidentally used eggnog instead of milk to make her mashed potatoes. She served them anyway, and everyone loved them. Nobody else knew her "secret recipe" was a mistake.

Gail Parker
Facebook

TRUE JOY OF COOKING

Family was thankful for Mom's tasty meals.

Born into a family of 12 children, Billye Peal Lumpkin (Mom) learned her way around the kitchen at an early age. At her mother's side, Billye began her lifelong journey of making delicious, creative meals.

When Mom married Dad in 1943, her most treasured wedding gift was Irma S. Rombauer's *The Joy of Cooking*. For the next 55 years, Mom, with her trusty book, prepared thousands of amazing meals and desserts for her family of six. The normal chattering of her four daughters disappeared at mealtime, replaced by quiet utterances of appreciation.

As for my favorite recipe, that would have to be the coconut cake decorated with seven-minute icing. She made it for my birthday every year. Not only was it beautiful, but it was pure JOY to eat. Thank you, Mom!

Edye Lumpkin Marvin
Pacific Grove, CA

Billye Lumpkin (right) fed her family with help from this well-thumbed *The Joy of Cooking*.

NOTEWORTHY MOM

She made sure they ate, even if she wasn't there to eat with them.

My mother, Anne Luedtke, was as selfless as they come. She worked as a chief cook at a restaurant from 4 to 11 p.m., then rose at 6 a.m. to wake us, prepare breakfast and get us off to school.

She also baked desserts before she went to work, as well as bread and rolls so Dad could have substantial sandwiches for lunch. She always made meals ahead of time for us to heat up when Dad returned from work.

We only saw Mom for about an hour after school, so every night I'd write her a short note and leave it on the kitchen table. Each morning I'd find a reply. I still have some of those notes, tied up in red satin ribbon. I'll never forget Mom's love for our family.

Barbara Robish South Milwaukee, WI

Barbara and her mom dressed up for church in 1950.

Judy's mother, Mary Schultz, was delighted to serve dinner on her new dishes, courtesy of a thoughtful *Ladies Home Journal* photographer that got to know the family.

Dishing Up for the Camera

Fake Thanksgiving came with a special gift of kindness.

Our family was selected for the "How America Lives" feature in *Ladies Home Journal* in 1948. The reporter and photographer arrived at the end of May and followed all of us (Mom, Dad, my brother, my sister and me) for a week, recording our every move. Everyone was pretty excited about it, especially in our town of 6,000, where things like this just didn't happen.

Since the article would be published in late October, we had to pretend it was already autumn. The reporter asked our mom to cook and serve a complete Thanksgiving meal. She told Mom to "go all out" and use her best holiday dishes.

Mom's face fell. She didn't want to admit that our best dishes weren't exactly the best, let alone suitable for a national magazine. While the reporter continued with her interview, the photographer quietly excused himself and slipped away for over an hour. When he came

back, he had a large box, which he placed on the floor, telling Mom to open it.

Her face lit up as if it were Christmas. Inside the box was a beautiful set of dishes, a service for 12 trimmed in gold, made by the Homer Laughlin China Co. There was even a soup tureen—something we kids had never seen before. Mom was near tears as she lovingly handled each piece.

When it came time to serve dinner, Mom walked slowly from the kitchen with the lovely new platter, which contained a small "turkey" (in reality, a large chicken).

Mom cherished those dishes and made sure they never saw the light of day unless it was a major event, though they were a must at every Thanksgiving.

I carry on the tradition, using the dishes for our Thanksgiving feast. But I serve a real turkey.

Judy Sikorski Rossford, OH

Since the article would be published in late

October, we had to pretend it was already autumn.

WHO'S READY FOR DESSERT?

Here is my mother, Jeannette Head, about to slice a homemade pie at a gathering
in 1986. Along with being a good cook, she had a wealth of home remedies.

Kathleen McDonald Erie, PA

MEMORABLE CELEBRATIONS

Birthdays and holidays are causes for togetherness and fun, with joyous parties, colorful Easter outfits, homemade Halloween costumes, DIY Christmas cards and more.

A Birthday to Remember

Mom pulled out all the stops when it came time to throw a party.

Sometimes I think if Martha Stewart had lived in my neighborhood in Kearney, Nebraska, as a little girl, she would have learned a thing or two simply by being a guest at my ninth birthday party in 1956. For this particular birthday, I was feted with a valentine theme.

My mother never met a paper plate or plastic cup that she liked. Ice cream was in crystal dishes set on pottery plates, and even my 2-year-old sister (bottom, at right) drank her chocolate milk out of a glass. Candles, pipe cleaner dolls (made by Mother) and valentine cutouts decorated the tables. Foil party hats decorated the guests. Hidden among the crowd is my other sister Marsha, age 10.

It was unthinkable that my mother would ever consider purchasing a bakery cake. She made an angel food cake, frosted with a confection that required sugar, egg whites, corn syrup, heat, a candy thermometer and an electric mixer. In the mid-1950s, children dressed in formal clothes for parties. My friend Linda Keiss (bottom, at left) wore a starched red dress with black velvet bows, and my brother Mark, age 6, looked comfortable in a necktie. My dress of polished cotton was made by my mother and featured covered buttons, embroidered yellow roses, scallops and piping on the collar.

My parents spent, without complaint, 3 cents on postage for each invitation that was mailed. We learned early in life that the most genuine form of invitation travels through the post office.

My mother's lasting gift to me was that, in addition to hosting my party (wearing high heels and a fashionable dress herself), she photographed the event with incomparable Kodachrome slide film. After all those years, the colors are so rich that I can almost taste the strawberry ice cream.

Aneeta Brown Washington, MO

It was unthinkable that my mother would ever consider purchasing a bakery cake.

Triple Celebration

My cousin Paul, sister Deb and I had July birthdays so my family drove to Denver, Colorado, and celebrated at Elitch Gardens. We're the ones in the hats. I'm seated second from left. I was 6 here, in 1962.
William Snesrud McPherson, KS

This little kitten sitting here
Brings lots of love
to Baby dear

HAPPY BIRTHDAY ONE YEAR OLD

Cute Kitty

This birthday card (above) was given to me on my first birthday, Nov. 5, 1929.
Mary Lou Boyd Haworth, NJ

Sharing a Special Day

I was born in 1943 on Oct. 10—my mom's birthday! A local newspaper ran this photo of my mother, Ruth, and me when I turned 2 and she turned 24.
John Wehrman Green Bay, WI

FIRST HIGHBALL

Her dad the bartender served it up straight.

I loved the New Year's Eve parties my parents usually hosted for our family when I was a kid growing up in the 1950s in Floral Park, New York. Some of my fondest holiday memories revolve around those fabulous house parties, which started in the living room and later moved down to our newly finished basement.

My older cousins, Rich and Freddie, were in a garage band and brought their instruments—a saxophone and a guitar. Uncle Carl played the drums, which were also carried down the basement stairs, much to the confusion of our dog, Poochie! Aunt Martha completed the quartet with her accordion.

Mom, who had been in a band in her teens, sometimes sat in on the saxophone, and everyone took a turn playing drums. I was 6 years old and thought everyone had live music in the basement on New Year's Eve!

While the band played, Dad handled bartending duties.

When I was old enough to stay up until midnight and saw everyone "ordering" drinks from him, I asked if I could have a highball.

Dad said, "Sure." He gave me a glass of ginger ale with a teaspoon of whiskey in it. I thought I was pretty grown-up, and it tasted good, too! So, I went back for another and another and another. After the first drink, Dad gave me nothing but straight ginger ale. Everyone thought this was cute, until I went back to school and told my first-grade teacher I had six highballs on New Year's Eve!
Alice Schuler Floral Park, NY

Alice's family rang in the new year together. She is the little girl in both photos.

Kelley loved Easter but hated dressing up in the girlish outfit her mom picked out for her in 1969 (near left). Wearing more casual attire during an outing with her parents in 1967, she's all smiles (far left).

Girl vs. Dress

She refused to wear the frilly ensemble Mom picked out for Easter.

Ever since I was little, I've hated dresses. My parents learned the true depth of my distaste on Easter weekend in 1969. Mom wanted a little baby she could dress up however she liked, but I had just turned 3 and was starting to resist. Most days I went along with her fussing over my hair and clothes, but for this particular Easter, she bought me a complete nightmare of an outfit.

This wasn't just a dress. This was a head-to-toe ensemble—a white dress with blue embroidery and flowery accents, accompanied by a bonnet with a blue ribbon that tied under my chin. If that wasn't bad enough, the outfit also included a matching baby blue wool coat that felt as comfortable as the prickly broom we used to sweep the garage. To complete my get-up, Mom added black patent leather shoes, a mini purse and white gloves.

All I really wanted was my Easter basket, so I usually tolerated wearing a dress for a little while in order to get it. But with this over-the-top outfit, I drew the line—I would not give in. Unfortunately, Dad and Papaw wouldn't give an inch either.

I ran around Mamaw and Papaw's living room like a panicked three-legged cat as Dad and Papaw wrestled with me for what seemed like forever. I kicked, screamed and cried, taking clothes off almost as fast as they struggled to put them back on me. In the end, it took two grown men more than two hours to get me back into that outfit.

The pictures from that day are priceless. My face was all red and puffy from crying, and I'm scowling as Papaw tries to wipe my tears away.

"I don't care if she ever wears a dress again!" Dad declared that day. Mission accomplished.

Kelley Jent Pendleton, IN

Sunday Lineup
We managed to get this picture of our kids Laura, 8; Christopher, 7; Michael, 6; Carolyn, 5; and Edward, 2, on Easter morning in 1971—before they scuffed their shoes and played in the grass.
Maureen Reid Little Silver, NJ

Spring 1964
Delighted with our Easter outfits, I, 8 (at left), laugh with my sisters Kathy, 11, and Sharon, 6, while awaiting a photo in Tucson, Arizona. Though our mother was an excellent seamstress, only my floral dress was one of her designs.
Peggy Oels Glendale, AZ

Dress Up, '70s Style
Every Easter before leaving for church, Mom had us pose in our new clothes in front of the family home in Eureka. In 1971, Dad, looking dapper, joined us for the picture. I'm in my lavender poncho outfit, with my sisters Linda (left) and Ginger in their minidresses.
Wendy Borgeson Windsor, CA

Party Time
Dressed in their Sunday best, these adorable kids carefully bring an egg-shaped cake to Easter festivities. My father, Charles Snyder, of Mansfield, Ohio, loved children and took this photo.
Ruth Fraley Show Low, AZ

LAMB CAKE LORE

Family traditions weren't dyed in the wool.

Making lamb cakes has been a tradition in my family ever since the 1920s, when my mother, Signe Jensen, brought a heavy cast-iron mold home to our small dairy farm.

I was 9 years old at the time and remember watching with great interest as she poured a raisin-studded batter into the lamb-shaped mold and baked it. After it was done, she carefully took the warm cake from the mold. Later she'd spread frosting on the lamb, then sprinkle some shredded coconut on top to give it a fluffy coat.

From then on, the lamb cake reappeared for special occasions, particularly Easter. But the little lamb was always so cute, no one wanted to eat it. So, instead, we would put it in a place of honor inside a glass cabinet until the coconut "wool" started to turn yellow.

I inherited my mom's treasured lamb mold when I became a mother myself. But instead of making the special cake only at Easter, I started my own family tradition with my son, Dennis. I baked him a lamb cake for his first birthday, surrounded it with

small candies and then set it all in front of him. He dug right in—literally! Dennis had so much messy fun with the cake that when my first daughter was born, I also made her a lamb cake of her very own.

The tradition lives on with my grandkids, who each get a lamb cake to dig their little fingers into on their first birthday. I'm not sure what my mom would think about how I turned her tradition on its head, but the kids definitely enjoy it!
Myrtle Hipke Racine, WI

Myrtle's grandsons, (from left) Nicholas and Brian, personally devoured their own lamb cakes on their first birthdays, per family tradition.

EASTER PARADE OF CROTEAUS — Easter was a beautiful day, and adding to the happiness of the day was the David Croteau family of Indigo Hill Road, Somersworth. The seven Croteau daughters (no boys) and their mother were dressed alike in outfits made by daughter Nola. From left to right are Brenda, 2; Kathy, 3; Donna, 8; Gail, 10; Paula, 13; Carol, 11; Nola, 16; mother Helen, and father David. (Democrat Photo-Meserve)

STYLISH SISTERS

They made the paper with new Easter dresses.

For most Easters, my six sisters and I would go up to our attic to see who fit into which hand-me-down dress. Then we'd spend an afternoon trying on hats, gloves and shoes.

Things changed in 1968. My oldest sister, Nola—who had plans to attend the School of Fashion Design in Boston—sewed matching Easter dresses for Mom and all of us girls. She picked a bright orange fabric and white lace for detailing down the front. We were all excited to wear our new finery.

Big families were much more common back then, but not many had seven girls and no boys, and that made ours newsworthy. The local paper ran a photograph of us in our matching dresses and Dad in his suit, capturing a wonderful family memory.
Paula Beyer Old Orchard Beach, ME

The Flicker Ladies
Janet, Pattie, Mom Margaret and Beverly wear look-alike Easter dresses in the early '60s. Mom and Beverly sewed the outfits. Dad dressed up after the picture was taken; he was always impeccably turned out.
Janet Moore Apex, NC

Dapper Duds

My brother Richard (right) and I always looked forward to Easter. We wore our new outfits to church, then got our baskets before going to our grandparents' in Baltimore, Maryland, for Easter dinner—and what a dinner! Here we are one Easter Sunday in the 1950s with our father, Leo Klug.
Martin Lee Klug Swanton, MD

Simply Adorable

The Andrews sisters (from left: Colleen, 2; me, 4; and Maureen, 3) and our brother Jim, 6, show off our mom's sewing skills in matching outfits in Coventry, Rhode Island, in 1962. We dressed alike for all holidays.
Kathleen Andrews Rochester Hills, MI

I treasure this picture of me (left) with my cousins Kathleen, Sandy, Cathy, Pam and Carol in our Easter finery in El Monte, California, in 1957. I still have that shawl and bonnet my Granny Catherine made for me.

Gail Perry Phelan, CA

THE SPARK OF A BAD IDEA

Fireworks are an outside activity for sure.

Imagine my excitement the day my father bought me three bundles of ladyfinger fireworks and a slew of sparklers. Since I was too young to use matches, I enlisted the help of my older sister Pat.

After lighting 20 or more sparklers over a couple of minutes, my sister grew weary of running outside every time I called to her. So the next time I asked for her help, she told me to come inside with my sparkler. I knew it wasn't a good idea, but Pat insisted that we light it in the kitchen. When I turned to head outside, the end of the lit sparkler brushed against a lace curtain. In seconds, the entire curtain was on fire. After a lot of yelling, my mother ran into the kitchen, pulled down the curtain, threw it into the sink and drenched it with water.

I was sent back outside with two books of matches.
John Whalen Walla Walla, WA

Patriotic Salute
Here I am with my sister Barb (dark hat) in Rochester, New York, on July 4, 1960. I was 4 and Barb was 5. We lived with our grandmother Helen Figler until 1962, when we moved two doors down. What great memories we share of those lovely days spent together!
Jean Yates Churchville, NY

Table Talk

My uncle John Court took this picture of the family enjoying a picnic in 1959. He left hundreds of slides of his family and friends, taken over more than 30 years throughout Washington state.
Carl Vincent Medical Lake, WA

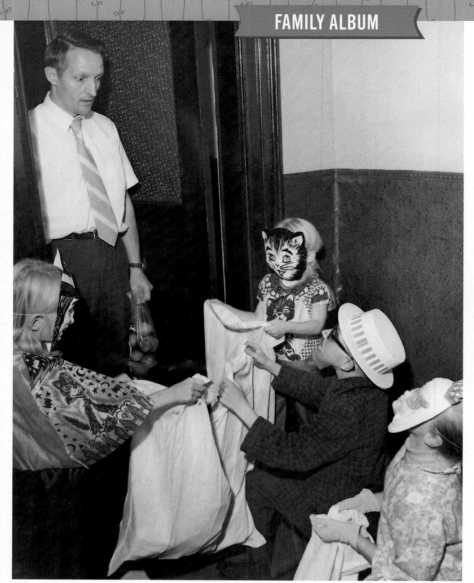

Too Cute to Spook
Our surprised dad, Royden Hunter, prepares to treat his four little monsters to fresh apples on Halloween in 1970.
Nina McLean

Show Yourself
In 1954, we lived on 42nd Street in Milwaukee, Wisconsin. My mother must have had some old sheets to spare, as she made me and my older brother Ken ghost costumes for Halloween. All went well until my brother donned his costume—I hadn't seen him put the costume on, so I refused to pose next to him for a photograph until I made sure that it was really him under the sheet. After taking a peek under it, I was satisfied and posed alongside him. Let the trick-or-treating begin!
Patricia Kasbohm Schley Fishers, IN

Definitely Most Original

Being a single mom and raising my daughter, Erin, on a very tight budget during the late 1970s, I needed to be creative with her Halloween costumes. Our town of Hicksville, New York, had a children's Halloween party, and almost every year, Erin would win the prize for most original costume. It rained the year she dressed up as the milk container, but she stayed nice and dry inside her cardboard carton. I fashioned the costumes so that she could wear a coat underneath and stay warm while she collected her goodies trick-or-treating.

Lisa O'Brien Campbell Hall, NY

Clowning Around

My wife, Margaret, made these costumes for our daughters Sandy and Linda. I snapped this as the girls were getting ready one Halloween around 1960.

Michael Lacivita Youngstown, OH

Karen dressed as Cinderella; her little brother, Evart, was a ghost; and her sister, Janice, was Little Red Riding Hood.

GIRLS, SHARE WITH YOUR BROTHER

For kids, the importance of candy cannot be underestimated.

It was so cold and rainy the Halloween of 1965 that we had to wear coats. What I remember most about it, though, was that it was my brother's worst Halloween ever.

He was short and had to run to keep up. All along the way, he dragged his paper trick-or-treat bag through every puddle. By the time we got home, there wasn't a single piece of candy left in his bag. He was in tears. So were my sister and I when Mom made us share our candy with him.
Karen Withers Millington, MI

One with the Costumes

My little brother and sister, Robbie and Aimee, dressed as Batman and a nurse for Halloween in 1968. They loved their costumes so much that they refused to take them off afterward. Aimee treated her doll patients with loving care.
Sarah Mason Plainfield, IN

One of a Kind

While living in Del Rio, Texas, my mom was a talented seamstress who sewed clothes for me and her granddaughters. In 1978 she made Halloween costumes for my daughters Sandy and Debbie using her own patterns. The girls looked forward to wearing the costumes that loving grandmother Opal Phillips made.
Carolyn Heep

Too Many Treats?

Pictured here are my younger siblings Peter and Laura tugging at Laura's yarn braids while celebrating Halloween 1964 in our uncle Don Brandt's den in Dearborn Heights, Michigan.
Sally Olson Harbor Springs, MI

CAST OF CLOWNS

Homemade costume made the rounds in this family.

Our oldest daughter was excited in October 1969 to go trick-or-treating with her family and friends. She was 1½ years old, and her great-grandmother wanted to make her a costume. What fun!

Gran, as we called her, had some shiny fabric that she thought would be perfect to use to make a clown outfit for her first great-granddaughter, Kristine. My husband, Jim, was Gran's oldest grandson.

The costume included black pompoms made from yarn and a hat that fit perfectly.

As our family grew, both our son, Jim Jr., and youngest daughter, Jacquelyn, wore the costume, as well as all eight of our grandchildren.

Today, Jacquelyn keeps the costume, well preserved and looking brand-new, at her home. Jim and I look forward to a time when our first great-grandchild will wear it.

Our entire family feels blessed to have this memory of Gran and her handiwork as part of our family history.
Eileen Mattison Hackettstown, NJ

(Top left) Kristine gives her brother a turn in the costume in 1972. (Top right) Gran ties the hat under great-granddaughter Kristine's chin. (Above) In 2002, Jim, Gran's oldest grandson, adds makeup on his granddaughter Brooke's nose.

HOLIDAY FOR ALL AGES

Halloween brings out specialty ads for adults and kids alike.

1953

TRICK OR TREAT?

Boasting with confidence, this ad suggests that you can trust the Old Gold cigarette brand, stating, "We're tobacco men…not medicine men."

1929

CHEWING THROUGH THE YEARS

During the mid-1940s, these impish cherubs wouldn't have been able to purchase their prized spearmint. Because of WWII rationing, Wrigley took its chewing gums off the civilian market and produced them solely for the U.S. Army.

Nov. 28, 1957 (left to right): Phil and Susie Keyes; my mother, Rosemary Lohr; my brother Chuck; Aunt Ethel Wurm; and Aunt Fan Conway enjoy Thanksgiving dinner together.

An Old-Fashioned Holiday

Everyone brought something to share on Thanksgiving.

The sweet smell of rhubarb pie mingled with the spicy aroma of pumpkin pie. A 20-pound fresh turkey roasted merrily in the cavernous electric roaster. The bacon sizzling in a frying pan on the stove foretold sweet-and-sour green beans. Mom was in her yellow gingham apron, bustling around the kitchen in all her glory.

From the living room TV, marching bands in the Macy's Thanksgiving Day Parade trumpeted the start of the holiday season. The old oak coffee table teemed with breakfast: hot buttery blueberry muffins, Cheerios, milk and orange juice—just enough to tide us over until dinner. As always, the parade featured a festive mixture of marching bands, majestic horses, clowns, huge floats and wonderful tethered character balloons all bobbing their way down the jam-packed streets of New York City.

As savory aromas wafted about the house, my sister and I were summoned to the kitchen to prepare our contribution: the relish tray. We gathered the vegetables and tools we needed. In addition to the olives, scallions and carrot sticks, we made celery-stick fans and radish roses, just as Mom had taught us.

The doorbell chimed, and the joyful chatter of relatives filled the house. Aunt Fan led the way in with her melt-in-your-mouth mashed potatoes, and Aunt Ethel followed with her bakery-perfect homemade cloverleaf rolls. Aunt Fan's daughter, Susie, and Susie's husband, Phil, brought up the rear, bearing a wicker cornucopia of fresh fruit.

The table was set with my grandmother's heirloom china—a delicate pattern of pink roses on white with a gold rim. The white linen napkins, crisp and freshly pressed, were folded into bishops' hats. Lead crystal glassware sparkled in the candlelight.

When everyone was assembled, the dinner was served: moist turkey; apple-chestnut dressing; maple sweet potatoes; creamy, rich mashed potatoes; sweet-and-sour green beans; red raspberry Jell-O salad; the relish plate; cloverleaf rolls; and gravy in my favorite china piece, the gravy boat.

Heads bowed around the table as we gave our thanks: "Bless us, O Lord, and these thy gifts, which we are about to receive from thy bounty, through Christ, our Lord. Amen."

The family feasted leisurely, and the conversation was lively. We all saved room for rhubarb pie or pumpkin pie topped with Mom's homemade whipped cream.

Ellen M. Lohr London, OH

Mama Ruth's Surprise Salad

Not every recipe is an instant classic.

Thanksgiving meant going to Aunt Ruth and Uncle Guy's house. My sister Annette and I called them Mama Ruth and Pawpaw as their grandchildren did. Instead of "over the river," our drive was only 12 miles of Texas highway to their farm outside Milano.

Watching the Macy's parade at home in Cameron usually made us last to arrive. Dinner was midday, and after an hour of chasing impatient men and children from the kitchen, Mama Ruth assembled us in the dining room for grace.

Our plates filled, all of us "kids"—between kindergarten and college age—sat at card tables on the sleeping porch. Graduating from the kids' table was a rite of passage, but the privilege could be revoked if the dining room couldn't hold all the grown-ups.

Thanksgiving fare was turkey cooked by Mama Ruth or her daughter Vae, Cousin John's cornbread dressing (or "cush") and ham made by my mother, Connie. Recipes were favorites from years of trial and error, but experiments turned up, courtesy of *Ladies' Home Journal* or a neighbor's sister-in-law's cousin who didn't know better.

Mama Ruth sometimes got flustered preparing for these get-togethers, leading to a few unintended results. One year Annette said, "There's banana in this potato salad." But the adults didn't seem to notice, and the kids kept Mama Ruth's mistake a secret.

After dinner, the kitchen became a beehive as leftovers were covered, put in the icebox or saved for the dog.

By midafternoon the rattle of dominoes, Cousin Chester's laughter and debates over Scrabble filled the house. The Aggies or Cowboys playing football added to the sounds. All the while, people who had sworn they wouldn't eat again for days trickled into the kitchen for bits of pie and cake.

Late in the afternoon, the remnants of dinner reappeared for a buffet supper. Festivities stretched into the night, but eventually the last car left as Mama Ruth and Pawpaw waved good night.

I've shared Thanksgivings with family and friends in different places over the years, but the clan in Milano is always together in my heart.

And if you're making fruit salad and potato salad at the same time this holiday, think of Mama Ruth—don't get flustered!

Ralph Cannon Denver, CO

Gathering for a Thanksgiving feast with Mama Ruth (back, far left) and Pawpaw (back, far right) was part of the natural order of things for Ralph (striped shirt).

Midcentury Memory

From the built-in buffet to the Lazy Susan on the table, this picture represents the wonderful '50s. My mother, Margie Condon, always cooked the biggest turkey she could find. Pictured from left are my mother; older sister Judy, 18; second big sister Midge, 14; and me, 12.
Phyllis Bebee Long Beach, CA

Gathered at the Table

Taken just before eating in 1959 in Elmira, New York, I'm in the red striped shirt between my maternal grandmother, "Mom" O'Herron, and my mother, Jean. Next to my mother are my aunt Dot O'Herron and my siblings Joy, Paul, Carol and Steve, who is shielding his eyes from the camera's flash. Flanking the cornucopia centerpiece are the turkey salt and pepper shakers that never missed a Thanksgiving.
Tom Huonker Rochester, NY

A FAMILY FEAST

Joy all around, no matter where one celebrates.

We would always have Thanksgiving at my grandfather's farm. All the sisters, one brother and their kids would show up. Aunt Louise always fixed a huge turkey in the wood-burning stove, and the rest of the sisters would take care of everything else. After the meal, some of the older guys watched TV while others hunted. We kids played touch football. Later on, all the kids drew names for Christmas gifts. I can still smell the coal-fired furnace and Grandpa smoking his cigars.

Jack Tiggleman
Facebook

I love Thanksgiving more than Christmas. We all get the gift of family and friends for whom we are truly thankful.

Rebecca Justine Walker
Facebook

There were only three of us—Mom, Dad and me—and we celebrated Thanksgiving differently: We ate out! Thanksgiving morning, I would watch all the parades on CBS, and then we would get dressed and go to a restaurant called Venetian Gardens. There were white tablecloths and napkins, salad forks

and crystal drinking goblets. Coats were taken into a cloakroom. There was a cigarette girl like you saw on TV, and a piano player played during dinner. We filled up on turkey, mashed potatoes and butternut squash. Later, we would go over to my grandfather's house for dessert. We ate out at a nice restaurant only twice a year, so it was a very special event.

Linda M. Young
Facebook

Thanks for Nothing

In 1954, our mother told my sister and me about Ragamuffin Day, an old Thanksgiving tradition when children dressed as hobos and went door to door, shouting, "This or that!" Neighbors were supposed to hand out food, fruits, canned goods or clothing. So off we went. But to our dismay, no one knew what to do when we shouted, "This or that!" We came home with nothing in our bags. And that was the end of "This or that!"

John Hoffman Wellington, FL

House to House

For Ragamuffin Day, we wore old clothes and Dad followed us around our New York City neighborhood, trying to be inconspicuous, while Mom cooked Thanksgiving dinner.

Sharon Schultz Glen Burnie, MD

Rudolph Speaks French?

Working with her mom playing the famous reindeer brought joy to many.

The 1980s bring up great memories of working as Rudolph, the red-nosed reindeer, with my mother and my sisters at our local mall. The mother of six, Mom has always been great with children.

The reindeer's hut was the size of a small shed, and it sparkled all over like it had just dropped from the North Pole. The front doors swung open to let a full-size reindeer head pop through; his nose was a red lightbulb that lit up whenever a button was pushed. A hand-operated lever moved the mouth, and we could twist the lever to make the eyes roll upward. We spoke through a microphone clipped to the reindeer head, and a burlap curtain allowed us to see out without anyone being able to see us inside.

I'd ask the children what they had on their Christmas lists or if they were ready for Christmas; I'd talk about anything the children wanted to, and then I'd ask them to touch my nose for some Christmas magic. Watching for when they'd touch the nose, I'd push the button, and it would light up a bright red.

When we needed a break, Mom came up with the great idea to say that Rudolph needed to have a "carrot break." We'd tell the children how important it was to have carrots and other vegetables, but that I (Rudolph) loved carrots most. We could take a 15-minute break to get a drink because days could be long when the lines of children were nonstop.

One year, Mom was visited by a little girl and her mother. Mom started with the usual greetings and questions, but the girl wouldn't say anything. She just looked at Rudolph. The girl's mother apologized to Rudolph, explaining that this little girl had just arrived from overseas and couldn't speak English. Then Mom heard the mother speak French to the little girl. Well, the woman jumped

back when Rudolph began speaking French to them! My mother is French Canadian, and although it's a different dialect, the little girl understood her well enough, and they had a great conversation. The scene was right out of *Miracle on 34th Street*! Even shoppers passing by began to notice that Rudolph was no longer speaking English, so they stopped to listen.

As soon as the little girl said goodbye to Rudolph, the mother went to the information booth to find the mall managers' office. She went there to thank them for having such a wonderful reindeer display. She told them what had happened with her daughter speaking French to Rudolph, and they had no idea that my mother could even speak another language. They were thrilled—and just as awed as the mother!

Mary J. Jones Falls Church, VA

When we needed a break, Mom came up with the great idea to say that Rudolph needed to have a "carrot break."

THE CARDBOARD-CUTOUT REINDEER

This classic Christmas character never gets old for the young at heart.

In 1948, when my father worked for the retailer Montgomery Ward in Hartford City, Indiana, cardboard-cutout Rudolphs were on display almost everywhere.

On Christmas Eve, my father brought two Rudolphs home, one for me (age 4) and one for my 9-year-old sister. We also received a pot-metal Rudolph bank with a slot in his back. Every time you inserted a coin, his nose lit up. I think I wore out the battery on the first day!

Today, one cardboard Rudolph lives on. My sister, who taught elementary school, set up the two Rudolphs in her classroom every Christmas until she retired. She gave the lone survivor to me. He was in bad shape, but I patched him back together with staples, tape, metal braces and a new red glass bulb for his nose. I still display Rudolph every Christmas for my grandchildren to enjoy. I hope someday they will pass him on to their own children and grandchildren.
Tim Kirkwood Kokomo, IN

Holiday Smiles

The Hightowers pose next to the tree at home in Dallas, Texas, in 1941. I am on the couch beside family friend Avon Yoakum (far left). In front are my sister Mae and brothers Karle and Bubba.
Ruby Wolford Dallas, TX

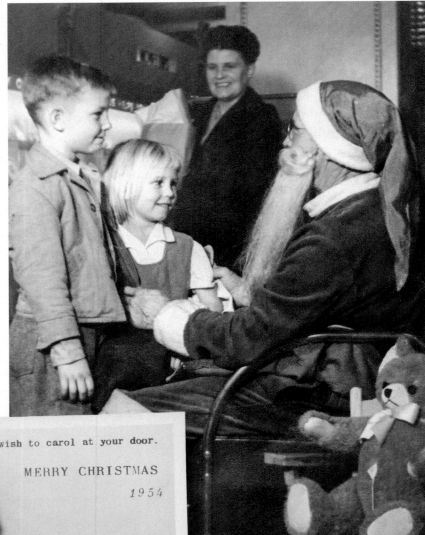

Real Dolls

This is my Uncle Ken and my mom, Barbara—yes, they were called Ken and Barbie—visiting Santa in 1946.
Andrea Tazelaar Crystal, MN

These three little notes wish to carol at your door.

MERRY CHRISTMAS
1954

Little Charmers

In 1954 I posed my children—Gail, Craig and Chris—in winter clothes for a sweet holiday card. They had a lot of fun with it.
Bernice Yunker Elba, NY

Christmas Happiness

Here I am enjoying Christmas in 1956 in Crystal, Minnesota, with the women in my life: my mother (far left), sister Marilyn and grandma.
Roland Anderson Minnetonka, MN

She's Making a List

My Christmas lists were mostly for practical things—clothes and some games. In 1962, I asked for red stretch slacks and a red-and-white blouse with patches, and I got them. I was 7 in this 1957 photo with my brother, Doug, 5, and sister, Phyllis, 3, showing off our Christmas presents in our house near Frontier, Michigan.
Ellyn Scarlett Elkhart, IN

Thanks, Grandma!

My grandma was an incredible seamstress. At Christmas my cousin Debbie (on the left) and I got new dolls with lovely wardrobes sewn from odd scraps and outgrown clothes on Grandma's Singer treadle machine.
Cindy Baier Boelk Oakfield, WI

CHRISTMAS TIME LAPSE

Grandpa shows his creative talent with DIY holiday greetings that focused on family.

Season's Greetings
The Knoppels · 1960

1966

Season's Greetings
The Knoppels · 1966

Family Photo Shoot

My grandpa, whom we called Pop-Pop, dreamed up Christmas card photo ideas for our growing family. Grandma Elsie (Nanny) helped keep the little ones' attention. We all posed as Pop-Pop patiently got the best shot. Then he developed the film in his basement darkroom. If we moved, he took more. He sent homemade greetings from 1941 to 1966, each with a different theme.

Darlene Knoppel Seilback Baldwin, MD

1947

1943

1955

1949

1943 Old-fashioned style was the year's theme. Nanny is wearing a feathered hat.

1947 Booties and cradles: Pop-Pop and Nanny get ready for grandkids.

1949 Joyce and I, the start of a new generation, learn about Santa.

1955 Pajamas, bare feet and Santa are part of the "Night Before Christmas" theme.

1960 Everyone hustles into place to take advantage of an unexpected snowy photo-op.

1966 Pop-Pop and Nanny's married children and eight grandchildren pose for one final shot.

WHAT WOULD DADDY SAY?

This is a Christmas card we made with the help of my husband's Uncle Fred, an amateur photographer. The photo was taken in 1952, when our daughter, Susan, was 3 and our son, Dana, was 2. The expressions on their faces show how really astonished they were to see "Mommy kissing Santa Claus" — aka me kissing my husband, Jack. It was taken around the time the song was so popular.

Barbara Larson Franklin, MA

The House in the Meadow

Shutta Crum

illustrated by **Paige Billin-Frye**

Albert Whitman & Company

Morton Grove, Illinois

For the best carpenters and electricians I know,
my brothers, Calvin and John Crum.
S.C.

To Giliah.
P. B-F.

Inspired by the poem "Over in the Meadow"
by Olive A. Wadsworth.

Crum, Shutta.
The house in the meadow / written by Shutta Crum ; illustrated by Paige Billin-Frye.
p. cm.
Summary: In the year following a couple's marriage, surrounded by their
ten best friends, different-sized crews of construction
workers build a house for them, from nine strong diggers to one inspector.
ISBN 0-8075-3393-9 (hardcover)
[1. House construction—Fiction. 2. Building—Fiction.
3. Construction workers—Fiction. 4. Counting. 5. Stories in rhyme.]
I. Billin-Frye, Paige, ill. II. Title. PZ8.3.C88643Ho 2003 [E]—dc21 2002011546

The design is by Carol Gildar.
The illustrations are paper collage with mixed media.

For more information about Albert Whitman & Company,
visit our web site at www.albertwhitman.com.

Over in the meadow, it was springtime when . . .

came a bride and a groom and their best friends **10**.
"And now…" said the couple. "A house!" said the **10**.
So they planned through the year, and when spring came again . . .

Over in the meadow, with a bucket big and fine,
shoveled Charlie with a backhoe and strong diggers **9**.

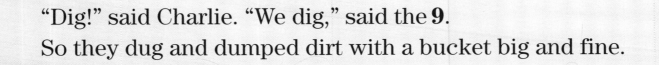

"Dig!" said Charlie. "We dig," said the **9**.
So they dug and dumped dirt with a bucket big and fine.

Over in the meadow, beside forms strong and straight,
Peter mixed concrete with his messy masons **8**.
"Pour!" said Peter. "We pour," said the **8**.
So they poured the concrete into forms strong and straight.

Over in the meadow, big carpenter Kevin
sawed up the lumber with his ready team of **7**.

"Build!" said Kevin. "We build," said the **7**.
So they built sturdy walls with carpenter Kevin.

Over in the meadow, at the spot marked with sticks,
worked Cindy with a rig and muddy drillers **6**.
"Drill!" said Cindy. "We drill," said the **6**.
So they drilled down for water at the spot marked with sticks.

Over in the meadow, with shingles by the drive,
climbed Calvin to the roof with his good roofers **5**.
"Hammer!" said Calvin. "We hammer," said the **5**.
So they hammered on the shingles that were stacked by the drive.

Over in the meadow, putting pipes through the floor,
Florence used her wrench and apprentices **4**.
"Plumb!" said Florence. "We plumb," said the **4**.
So they joined all the pipes going through the new floor.

Over in the meadow, testing lights carefully,
wired John the electrician and his trained crew of **3**.
"Connected?" asked John. "Connected!" said the **3**.
So they switched on the power in the house carefully.

Over in the meadow, in the last room to do,
Kellie rolled on paint with her new helpers **2**.
"Use blue," said Kellie. "For the baby!" said the **2**.
So they used the blue paint in the last room to do.

Over in the meadow, to see if everything was done,
came the top town official with Inspector Number **1**.
"Look!" said the husband. "I'll look," said the **1**.
So he looked and he listed. Everything was done!

book has a theme, just to make it more fun. Try to think up a theme of your own, and choose recipes that go with it. How about a menu of foods that can be eaten with your fingers? Why not serve a meal honoring some of your favorite Christmas characters? (Be sure to put Frosty the Snowball on your list.) Or forget about planning a meal, and make a variety of desserts instead. Anything is possible!

Be sure to share your masterpiece with someone else. Whether you make one dish or an entire meal, half the fun of cooking is watching someone else enjoy the food.

CRAFTS

Like the recipes, all of the crafts in this book are easy to make, but some are easier than others. If you haven't tried making crafts before, start with something easy, like a Teeny Tiny Tree or Rocky and Rita Reindeer. As you gain confidence, put together a Yuletide Angel or a Happy Holidays Wreath. Once you've tackled these crafts, you're ready to make a Merry Christmas Tree.

Don't be afraid to use your imagination when decorating your crafts. Use markers, colored construction paper, scraps of fabric, or even glitter to give your crafts a personal touch.

Cooking Smart

Christmas is a time for surprises, but you don't want them to happen while you're cooking. Whether you are a new or experienced cook, these cooking tips can help you avoid a kitchen disaster.

BEFORE YOU COOK

- Get yourself ready. If you have long hair, tie it back to keep it out of the food, away from flames, and out of your way. Roll up your sleeves, and put on an apron. And be sure to wash your hands well with soap.
- Read through the entire recipe and assemble all of the ingredients. It's no fun to find out halfway through a recipe that you're out of eggs.
- Go through the recipe with an adult helper and decide which steps you can perform yourself and which you'll need help with.

WHILE YOU COOK

- Raw meat and raw eggs can contain dangerous bacteria. Wash your hands and any utensils or cutting boards you've used after handling these raw foods. Never put cooked meat on an unwashed plate that has held raw meat. Any dough that contains raw eggs isn't safe to eat until it's cooked.
- Keep cold foods in the refrigerator until you need them.
- Wash fruits and vegetables thoroughly before using them.
- Turn pot handles to the back of the stove so the pots won't be knocked off by accident. When you are taking the lid off a hot pan, always keep the opening away from your face so the steam won't burn you.
- Use a potholder when handling

hot pans. Be sure the potholder is dry before you use it. The heat from the pan will come right through a wet potholder.

- Always turn off the stove or oven as soon as you're done with it.
- Be careful with foods when they come out of the microwave. Although they may seem to be cool to the touch, microwaving can produce hot spots. When you're heating a liquid in the microwave, stir it often to distribute the heat evenly.
- Only use microwave-safe dishes in the microwave. Never put anything metal in the microwave.
- Don't cut up food in your hand, use a cutting board.
- Carry knives point down.
- Be careful when opening cans. The edges of the lids are very sharp.
- Don't save the mess for the end. Try to clean up as you go along.

AFTER YOU COOK

- Once you've finished cooking, be sure to store your creation in the refrigerator if it contains any ingredients that might spoil.
- Be a courteous cook: clean up your mess. Leave the kitchen looking as clean as (or cleaner than) you found it.

SOME CRAFTY TIPS

Assembling a craft is a lot like cooking, and many of the same tips apply. Read the instructions and gather your supplies before you start. Play it safe with your supplies, especially scissors, and be sure to get an adult friend to help you when you need it. Put down newspapers to protect your work surface. And, of course, be sure to clean up your mess when you're done.

After Caroling

Christmas Tree Tostada

▼

Chill-chasing Cider

▼

Rudolph's Peanut Butter
Oat Treats

▼

Chocolate-dipped Apple Slices

▼

Fantastic Fudge

▼

Teeny Tiny Tree

Christmas Tree Tostada

YOU WILL NEED:

1 pound hamburger

1 package taco seasoning mix
(enough for 1 pound hamburger)

6 small flour tortillas

1 green pepper, seeded and diced

1 tomato, diced

½ cup sliced black olives

½ cup sliced green olives

6 ounces sliced Monterey Jack cheese,
cut into strips

3 cups shredded lettuce

sour cream

taco sauce

1. Preheat oven to 350°.

2. Prepare hamburger with taco seasoning mix, according to package directions.

3. Cut tortillas into tree shapes as shown, discarding the shaded areas.

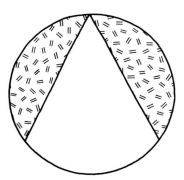

4. With a spoon, spread ⅓ cup hamburger mixture evenly over each tortilla. Leave a ½-inch border of tortilla all the way around each tostada.

5. Use green pepper, tomatoes, and olives to decorate tostadas like Christmas trees.

6 Arrange the cheese on each tostada in a zigzag pattern to make a garland.

7 Use a spatula to place tostadas on a baking sheet. (You will probably be able to bake two at a time.) Bake for 5 to 7 minutes or until cheese is melted.

8 Place tostadas on serving plates. Arrange lettuce at the bottom of each tostada to make a tree skirt.

9 Serve tostada with sour cream and taco sauce.

Serves 6

Chill-chasing Cider

YOU WILL NEED:

³/₄ **cup apple juice or apple cider**

¹/₄ **cup orange juice**

1 cinnamon stick

Combine ingredients in a small saucepan and stir. Cook over medium heat for about 5 minutes or until juice is warm. Pour into a mug and serve.

To microwave, combine juices in a microwave-safe mug and stir. Place cinnamon stick in mug and microwave on high for 1 minute and 30 seconds or until warm. Stir before serving.

Serves 1

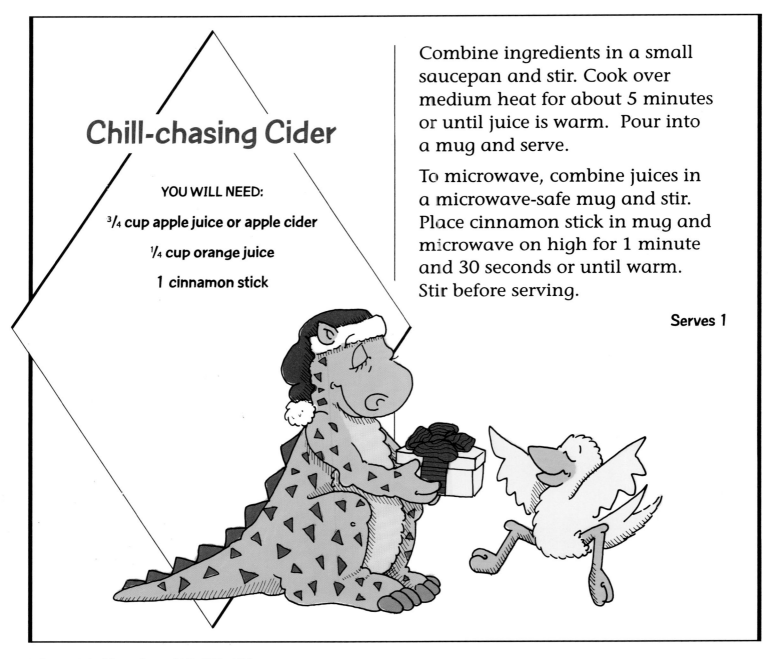

Rudolph's Peanut Butter Oat Treats

YOU WILL NEED:

¼ cup butter or margarine, melted

⅓ cup peanut butter

½ cup brown sugar

1 cup oatmeal (not instant)

1 In a medium bowl, combine melted butter, peanut butter, and brown sugar. Stir well.

2 Add oatmeal and stir well.

3 With your hands, roll oatmeal mixture into 1-inch balls and place on waxed paper.

Makes 20 treats

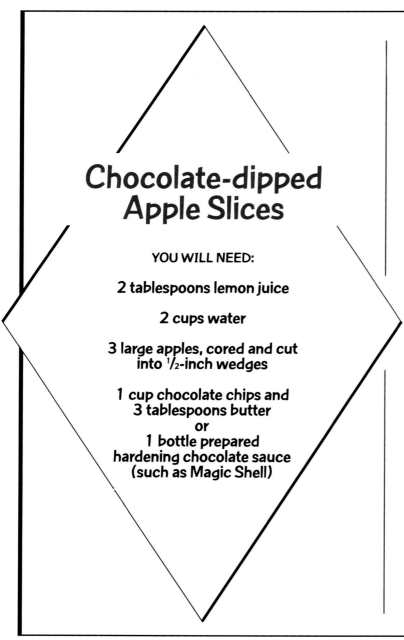

Chocolate-dipped Apple Slices

YOU WILL NEED:

2 tablespoons lemon juice

2 cups water

3 large apples, cored and cut into $\frac{1}{2}$-inch wedges

1 cup chocolate chips and 3 tablespoons butter
or
1 bottle prepared hardening chocolate sauce (such as Magic Shell)

1 Line a baking sheet with waxed paper.

2 In a large bowl, combine lemon juice and water. Place apples in lemon juice mixture. Toss to coat apples with lemon juice mixture. Set aside.

3 If you don't have a microwave, skip this step and use hardening chocolate sauce instead. Place chocolate chips and butter in a microwave-safe dish. Microwave on high for 1 minute. Stir well. If chocolate is not completely melted, microwave on high for 20 seconds more and stir. Repeat until chips are melted.

4 Place apple slices on a paper towel and pat dry with another paper towel.

⑤ If you made your own chocolate sauce, dip apple slices halfway into chocolate mixture and place on baking sheet. If you are using hardening chocolate sauce, arrange apple slices on baking sheet and drizzle with chocolate.

⑥ Refrigerate apple slices for about 1 hour or until chocolate has set.

Makes 30 apple slices

If the chocolate mixture begins to set before you are finished dipping the apples, microwave on high for about 20 seconds and stir.

Holiday Greetings Around the World

You could say "Merry Christmas" or "Happy Holidays," but why not try something new? Here's how to make your Christmas greetings the international way. The pronunciations are included so you can give it a try.

German: Fröhliche Weihnachten (FRUH-lihsh-eh VY-nahkh-tehn)
French: Joyeux Noël (zhwah-YUH noh-EHL)
Swedish: God Jul (GOO-D YEE-ool)
Italian: Buon Natale (BWOHN nah-TAHL-ay)
Spanish: Feliz Navidad (fay-LEES nah-vee-DAHD)
Polish: Wesolych Swiat (veh-SOH-wihkh shvee-OHNT)
Russian: S Rozhdestvom Kristovym (s'rahzh-dyehst-VOOM hkrees-TOH-vm)

Fantastic Fudge

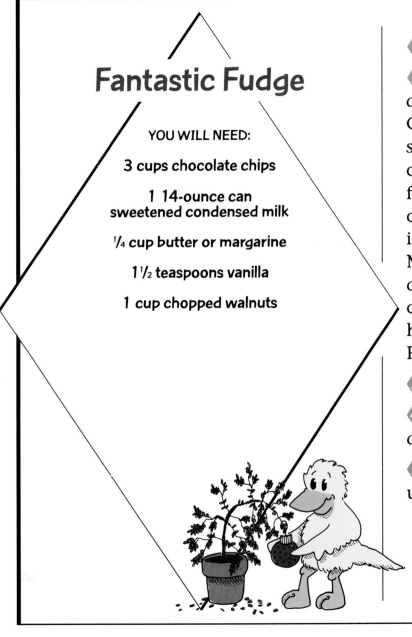

YOU WILL NEED:

3 cups chocolate chips

1 14-ounce can
sweetened condensed milk

¼ cup butter or margarine

1½ teaspoons vanilla

1 cup chopped walnuts

1. Grease an 8- by 8-inch pan.

2. Combine chocolate chips, milk, and butter in a medium saucepan. Cook over medium-low heat, stirring constantly, until chocolate chips are melted. Remove pan from heat. To microwave, place chocolate chips, milk, and butter in a microwave-safe dish. Microwave on high for 2 minutes and stir. If chocolate is not completely melted, microwave on high for 20 seconds more and stir. Repeat until chips are melted.

3. Stir in vanilla and walnuts.

4. Pour chocolate mixture into pan and smooth with a spoon.

5. Refrigerate for about 1 hour or until set. Cut into small squares.

Makes 49 to 64 pieces

Teeny Tiny Tree

YOU WILL NEED:

pencil

ruler

construction paper
(green, brown, red, and yellow)

scissors

white liquid glue

tracing paper

1 3½-inch piece of thread

paper punch

8 inches of ⅛-inch wide
red ribbon

1 7-inch piece of gold
elastic cord (optional)

◆ Draw a 1- by 11-inch strip on green construction paper and cut it out.

◆ Measure in 1 inch from one end of the strip and draw a faint pencil line across the strip. Measure in 2 inches from the same end of the strip and draw another faint pencil line. Repeat on the other end of the strip.

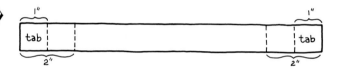

◆ Fold the strip in half the short way.

◆ Fold the two ends of the strip in on the lines that are 2 inches from the end.

◆ Fold the two ends of the strip back out again on the line that is

1 inch from the end. These last 1-inch sections are the tabs.

THE TRUNK:

1 Draw a 1- by 5-inch strip on brown construction paper and cut it out.

2 Measure in 1 inch from one end of the strip and draw a line across the strip. Repeat at 2, 3, and 4 inches from the end. The paper will be divided into five 1-inch sections.

3 Fold on each of the lines, always keeping the line on the inside of the fold.

4 Overlap the two end sections and glue them together to form a three-dimensional square.

TO ASSEMBLE:

Apply glue to the outside of the tree tabs and slide them into the trunk. Hold them in place until the glue sets.

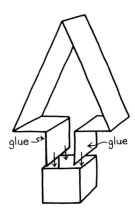

TO DECORATE:

1 Place tracing paper on top of figures A and B below and trace. Cut out tracing paper patterns. Place heart pattern on red construction paper and trace.

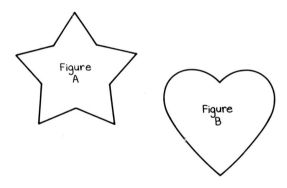

Place star pattern on yellow construction paper and trace. Cut out construction paper star and heart.

2 Glue the heart to one end of the thread and the star to the other. Allow glue to dry.

3 Pinch the top of the tree together and punch a hole through both layers of paper with a paper punch.

4 Slide the ribbon through the holes. Pull the thread with the heart and star through the space between the ribbon and the top of the tree as shown.
Tie the ribbon into a bow.

You can make your Teeny Tiny Tree into a napkin holder. Make a hole on each side of the trunk with a paper punch. Then thread a 7-inch piece of gold elastic cord through the holes and tie it around a rolled napkin.

The Colors of Christmas

Crunchy Paprika Chicken
▼
Great Greeny Beanies
▼
Easy Elfin Rice
▼
Frosty the Snowball
▼
*Happy Holidays
Wreath*

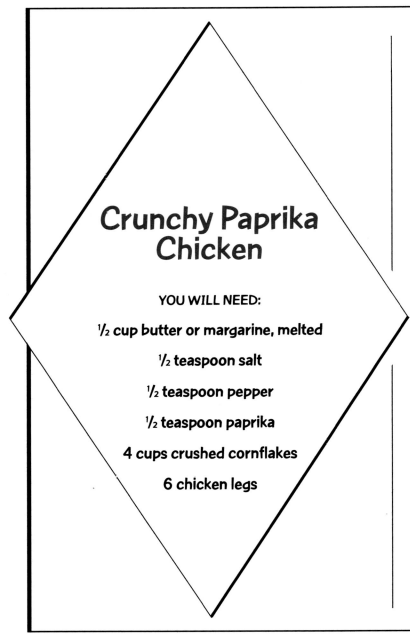

Crunchy Paprika Chicken

YOU WILL NEED:

½ cup butter or margarine, melted

½ teaspoon salt

½ teaspoon pepper

½ teaspoon paprika

4 cups crushed cornflakes

6 chicken legs

1. Preheat oven to 375°.

2. In a shallow bowl, combine melted butter, salt, pepper, and paprika. Stir well.

3. Place cornflakes in a second shallow bowl.

4. Dip chicken in butter mixture and then roll in cornflakes.

5. Arrange chicken on a baking sheet. Don't let the chicken pieces touch each other.

6. Bake for 50 minutes.

Serves 6

Great Greeny Beanies

YOU WILL NEED:

1 1-pound package frozen french-cut green beans, thawed

1 10½-ounce can cream of mushroom soup

½ cup shredded cheddar cheese

¾ cup french fried onions

1 Preheat oven to 375°.

2 Combine beans, soup, and cheese in a casserole dish. Stir well.

3 Sprinkle french fried onions over beans.

4 Bake for 25 minutes or until beans are bubbly in the center.

Serves 6

St. Lucia Day

In Sweden, the Christmas season begins on December 13, St. Lucia Day. On this day, the oldest daughter in each family gets up very early in the morning to perform a special duty. She puts on a long white dress, and she takes a wreath holding seven lit candles and places it on her head. Then she awakens her family with a song and serves them a breakfast of coffee and saffron buns.

Easy Elfin Rice

YOU WILL NEED:

2 tablespoons butter

1 cup uncooked long grain rice (not instant)

1 10½-ounce can chicken broth

1 10½-ounce can french onion soup

2 tablespoons chopped pimento (optional)

1. Preheat oven to 400°.

2. Combine ingredients in a casserole dish.

3. Bake for 40 minutes or until rice is tender and liquid is absorbed.

Serves 6

For milder-flavored rice you can substitute one can of water for the onion soup.

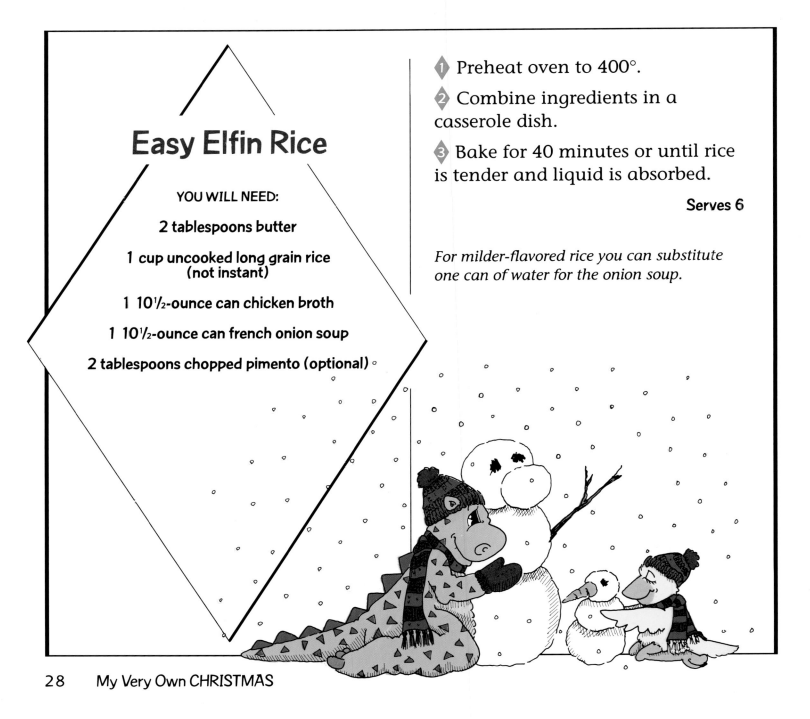

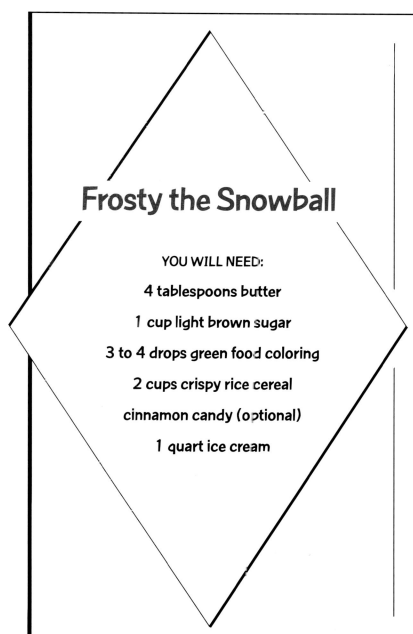

Frosty the Snowball

YOU WILL NEED:

4 tablespoons butter

1 cup light brown sugar

3 to 4 drops green food coloring

2 cups crispy rice cereal

cinnamon candy (optional)

1 quart ice cream

1 Line a baking sheet with waxed paper.

2 Melt butter in a large saucepan over medium-low heat. Add sugar and stir to dissolve. Remove from heat.

3 Add three to four drops of green food coloring and stir well.

4 Add cereal and stir gently.

5 Spoon cereal mixture onto waxed paper and divide into four pieces. Form each piece into a wreath. If you like, decorate the wreaths with cinnamon candy.

6 Refrigerate wreaths for about 1 hour or until set. Before serving, place a scoop of ice cream in the middle of each wreath.

Serves 4

Happy Holidays Wreath

YOU WILL NEED:

1 9- by 12-inch piece of
green construction paper

ruler

pencil

pinking shears or regular scissors

white liquid glue

1 4-inch piece gold tinsel pipe cleaner

small thread spool

clear-drying glue (look for Super Tacky
glue in sewing and craft stores)

1 15-inch piece red satin ribbon

red sequins

gold spray paint
(optional)

1 Fold the construction paper in half the long way. Unfold paper and fold each half of the paper in half. Make a crease.

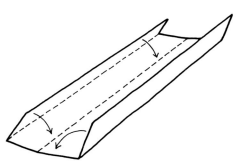

2 Unfold paper and refold it in half as in step 1. Place a ruler along the folded side of the paper and make a dot every ½ inch. Using pinking shears or regular scissors, cut at each dot from the folded edge to the crease.

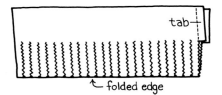

tab

folded edge

3 Cut the last strip off to make the connecting tab.

4 Unfold the paper. Overlap the two uncut sections to make a triangular tube. Glue the two sections together with white liquid glue.

5 Form the triangular tube into a circle, and glue the tab to the inside of the wreath with white liquid glue.

tab

6 Wrap about 2 inches of the pipe cleaner around a pencil to make a coil. Slide the pencil out. Tuck the straight end of the pipe cleaner into the hole in the spool to make a candle with a flame.

7 Glue the bottom of the spool to the inside of the wreath with clear-drying glue.

8 Thread the ribbon behind two strips at the bottom of the wreath and tie a bow.

9 Glue sequins to the wreath with clear-drying glue.

You can have an adult helper spray paint the spool gold if you like.

Santa Supper

Stroganoff St. Nick

▼

Pear Mouse

▼

Mrs. Claus's Favorite Lime Pie

▼

Rocky and Rita Reindeer

Stroganoff St. Nick

YOU WILL NEED:

3 pounds round steak, cut into bite-size pieces

2 10½-ounce cans cream of mushroom soup

1 envelope dried onion soup mix (not single serving)

¾ cup water

2 cups sour cream

8 cups cooked egg noodles or rice

1. Preheat oven to 350°.

2. Grease a 3-quart baking dish.

3. Combine meat, cream of mushroom soup, onion soup, and water in baking dish. Stir well.

4. Cover and bake for 1 hour or until center is bubbly and meat is no longer pink in the middle.

5. Remove from oven, and stir in sour cream.

6. Serve over noodles or rice.

Serves 6 to 8

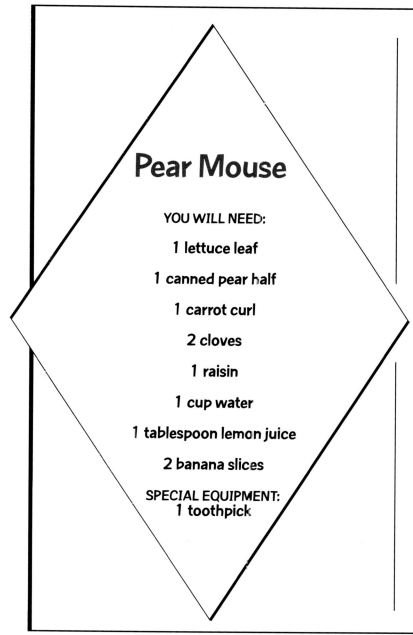

Pear Mouse

YOU WILL NEED:

1 lettuce leaf

1 canned pear half

1 carrot curl

2 cloves

1 raisin

1 cup water

1 tablespoon lemon juice

2 banana slices

SPECIAL EQUIPMENT:
1 toothpick

1. Place lettuce leaf on serving plate.

2. Place pear, rounded side up, on lettuce leaf. The small end of the pear is the head of the mouse.

3. Insert carrot curl under large end of pear to make the tail.

4. Press cloves into small end of pear to make the eyes.

5. Position raisin underneath eyes to make the nose.

6. In a small bowl, combine water and lemon juice. Dip banana slices in lemon juice mixture to keep them from turning brown.

7. Break toothpick in half. Insert one end of broken toothpick into side of banana slice. This will be an ear. Insert other end of toothpick in pear to attach banana to the side of the mouse's head. Repeat with second banana slice.

Makes 1 Pear Mouse

Mrs. Claus's Favorite Lime Pie

YOU WILL NEED:

1 6-ounce can limeade, thawed

1 14-ounce can sweetened condensed milk

2 cups whipped topping

1 prepared graham cracker crust

sliced strawberries for garnish (optional)

1 In a medium bowl, stir together limeade and milk.

2 Fold in whipped topping.

3 Pour lime mixture into pie crust and smooth with a spoon. Decorate with strawberry slices.

4 Refrigerate for about 2 hours before serving.

Serves 6 to 8

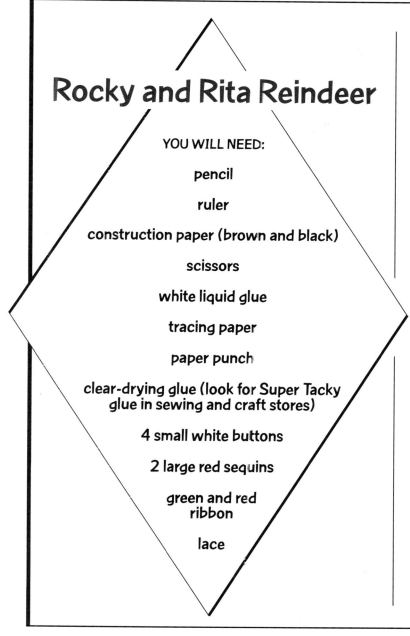

Rocky and Rita Reindeer

YOU WILL NEED:

pencil

ruler

construction paper (brown and black)

scissors

white liquid glue

tracing paper

paper punch

clear-drying glue (look for Super Tacky glue in sewing and craft stores)

4 small white buttons

2 large red sequins

green and red ribbon

lace

THE BODY:

1. Draw a 3- by 6-inch rectangle on brown construction paper. Cut it out.

2. Fold the rectangle in half the short way.

3. Unfold the paper and fold each half of the rectangle in half.

4. Unfold the paper. The folds will have divided the paper into four sections. Overlap the two end sections and glue them together with white liquid glue to make a triangular tube.

glue

5. Repeat steps 1 through 4 to make a second body.

THE HEAD:

1 Draw a 6- by 8-inch rectangle on brown construction paper. Cut it out.

2 Fold rectangle in half the short way. Set aside.

3 Place tracing paper on top of figure C on page 39 and trace. Cut out tracing paper pattern.

4 Place the pattern on the folded construction paper, with the dotted edge on the fold. Trace around the pattern.

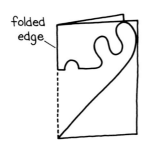

folded edge

5 Without unfolding the construction paper, cut out the head. You will cut through both layers of construction paper. Unfold the paper.

6 Repeat steps 1 through 5 to make a second head.

TO ASSEMBLE:

1 At one of the corners of one of the bodies, measure 1½ inches from the bottom and make a faint pencil mark.

2 Use white liquid glue to glue the head to the body, with the tip of the nose at the pencil mark.

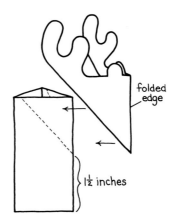

folded edge

$1\frac{1}{2}$ inches

3 Repeat steps 1 and 2 to assemble the second reindeer.

TO DECORATE:

1 Use a paper punch to punch four circles out of black construction paper. Glue the four circles to the centers of four white buttons with clear-drying glue. Then glue the eyes to the reindeer's heads with clear-drying glue.

2 Attach the red sequin noses with clear-drying glue.

3 Decorate Rocky and Rita with ribbons and lace attached with clear-drying glue.

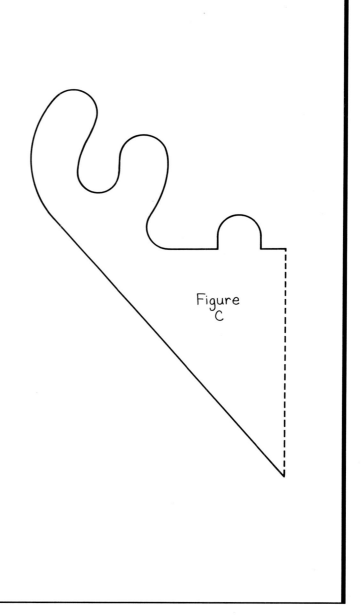

Figure
C

Cozy Christmas Breakfast

Ho-Ho-Holiday Omelet
▼
Cheery Hot Chocolate
▼
The Best Cinnamon Bread
▼
*Merry Christmas
Tree*

Ho-Ho-Holiday Omelet

YOU WILL NEED:

6 eggs

½ cup milk

1 cup shredded cheese

½ teaspoon salt

⅛ teaspoon pepper

ADDITIONAL INGREDIENTS (OPTIONAL):

½ cup chopped ham

3 tablespoons chopped onion

3 tablespoons chopped green pepper

3 tablespoons chopped tomato

¼ cup sliced mushrooms

3 tablespoons chopped black olives

1. Preheat oven to 375°.

2. Grease a 9- by 9-inch square baking pan or a 9-inch round baking pan.

3. In a medium bowl, beat eggs with a fork.

4. Add milk, cheese, salt, and pepper and stir well.

5. Stir in as many additional ingredients as you like.

6. Pour egg mixture into baking pan. Bake for 30 to 40 minutes or until eggs are completely set. The more additional ingredients you add, the longer the omelet will take to cook.

Serves 4

Christmas Carol Charades

All you need to play this game is from 2 to 10 people, a pencil and some paper, and a lot of imagination. To prepare for the game, cut or tear a large piece of paper into 10 pieces. Then copy each of the following Christmas carols onto a piece of paper.

Rudolph the Red-nosed Reindeer
Silent Night
Jingle Bells
Frosty the Snowman
White Christmas
Carol of the Bells
O Little Town of
**   Bethlehem**
We Wish You a Merry
**   Christmas**
Santa Claus is
**   Coming to Town**
O Christmas Tree

Tightly fold up each piece of paper, and drop it into a large bowl. Now you're ready to play.

To begin with, an adult helper reads the list of Christmas carols aloud. Then the first player draws a slip of paper from the bowl and looks at it without showing it to any of the other players. (You might want to have your adult helper standing by for reading help.) Without talking, the player must try to get the other players to say the name of the Christmas carol on the paper. The player can fly like a reindeer or jingle imaginary bells, but he or she must not make a sound.

Continue to play until everyone has had at least one turn and you've guessed all the Christmas carols.

Cheery
Hot Chocolate

YOU WILL NEED:

2 tablespoons chocolate syrup

1 ¼ cups milk

1 large marshmallow or
1 teaspoon creamy peanut butter

Combine ingredients in a small saucepan. Cook over medium heat, stirring constantly, until hot chocolate is warm. Pour into a mug and serve.

To microwave, combine chocolate syrup and milk in a microwave-safe mug. Microwave on high 1 minute. Add marshmallow or peanut butter. Microwave on high 30 to 40 seconds longer. Stir before serving.

Serves 1

The Best Cinnamon Bread

YOU WILL NEED:

³/₄ cups butter or margarine, melted

1¹/₃ cups brown sugar

1 teaspoon cinnamon

1 teaspoon vanilla

3 cans buttermilk refrigerator biscuits
(10 biscuits per package)

1 cup chopped pecans

SPECIAL EQUIPMENT:
Bundt pan

1. Preheat oven to 350°.

2. Grease Bundt pan.

3. In a small bowl, combine melted butter, brown sugar, cinnamon, and vanilla. Stir until sugar is dissolved. Set aside.

4. Separate biscuits. Cut each biscuit into quarters.

5. Sprinkle ⅓ cup pecans in bottom of pan. Arrange ⅓ of biscuit pieces on top of pecans. (Biscuits will be crowded.) Pour ⅓ of syrup mixture over biscuits. Repeat the layers two more times.

6. Bake for 30 to 40 minutes or until toothpick inserted in a biscuit comes out clean.

Serves 8

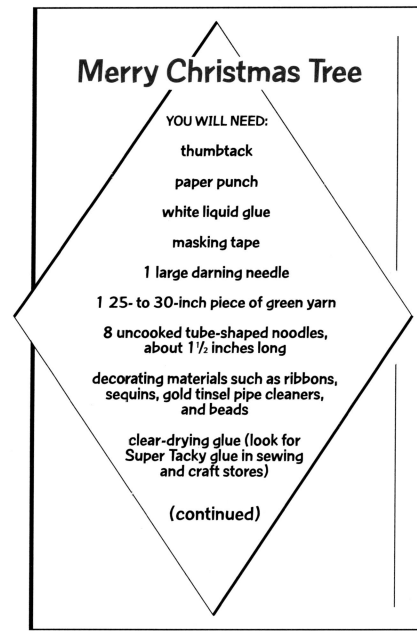

Merry Christmas Tree

YOU WILL NEED:

thumbtack

paper punch

white liquid glue

masking tape

1 large darning needle

1 25- to 30-inch piece of green yarn

8 uncooked tube-shaped noodles, about 1½ inches long

decorating materials such as ribbons, sequins, gold tinsel pipe cleaners, and beads

clear-drying glue (look for Super Tacky glue in sewing and craft stores)

(continued)

THE TREE:

1 Arrange the four pieces of green construction paper in a rectangle as shown below. With masking tape, tape the four pieces of paper together without overlapping them.

2 Place the rectangle so the narrow ends are at the sides. Draw a line across the rectangle 6 inches from one side. Draw another line across the rectangle 6 inches from the other side. Cut across the rectangle on each of the two lines to make the rectangle into a square. Set square aside for now.

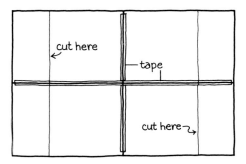

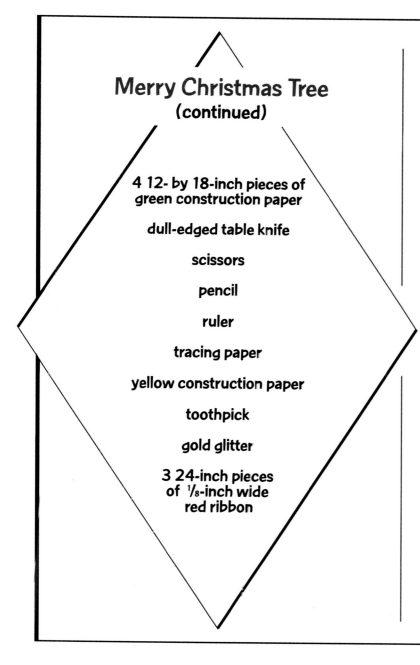

Merry Christmas Tree
(continued)

4 12- by 18-inch pieces of
green construction paper

dull-edged table knife

scissors

pencil

ruler

tracing paper

yellow construction paper

toothpick

gold glitter

3 24-inch pieces
of ⅛-inch wide
red ribbon

3 Take one of the pieces of paper you cut off from the rectangle and draw a 4½- by 12-inch rectangle on it. Cut out the rectangle.

4 Measure in 2¼ inches along one of the narrow ends of the rectangle and make a dot. With a ruler, draw a diagonal line connecting the dot to one of the bottom corners as shown. Repeat with the other corner. Cut out the section that is shaded in the diagram. You will have formed a triangle.

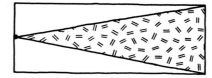

5 Place the square you made in step 2 in front of you so the tape is facing up. Place the triangle along one of the seams of the square and trace around it. Place the triangle alongside the triangle you just drew and trace around it again. Continue until you have come around again to the original triangle. You will have divided the square into 16 pie-shaped sections.

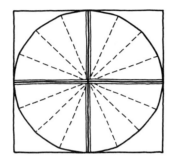

⑥ Cut along the outside of the triangles to form a 16-sided circle.

⑦ You will need to score the lines you have just drawn to make the folding easier. Using a dull-edged table knife, place your ruler edge on each line and gently run the

knife from top to bottom. Do not cut or tear the paper.

⑧ Cut along one of these scored lines just to the center point and stop.

⑨ Start at the first section next to the line you just cut and fold the first section on top of the second section along the scored lines. Turn the paper over and fold the first and second section on top of the third section along the scored line. Continue to fold back and forth, like a fan, until you have run out of paper.

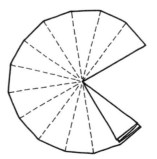

TO ASSEMBLE:

1 Place the folded triangle in front of you with the point facing up. Find the side of the triangle with the pencil marks. Measure in ½ inch from this side and make a faint line. Measure up ¾ inch from the bottom of the triangle and make a faint line. Make a dot where these two lines cross.

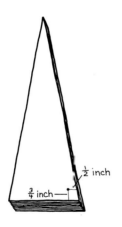

2 Have an adult helper push a sharp thumbtack through the dot, pushing it through all the layers of paper. Remove the thumbtack.

3 Unfold the piece of paper. Tape the cut you made in step 8 back together with masking tape to form a complete circle.

4 You will see small pinpricks all the way around the circle. Center a paper punch over each one of these pinpricks and punch out a hole.

5 Place the circle in front of you with the pencil lines facing down. Pull the center of the circle upward to form a cone.

6 Thread the yarn onto the needle. Turn the cone on its side so you can see underneath it. You will see eight pairs of holes, one pair in each inside fold of the cone. Push the needle through one pair of holes and pull about half of the length of yarn through the holes.

7 Thread a noodle over the needle and onto the yarn to act as a spacer. Push the needle through the next pair of holes and thread a second noodle onto the yarn. Continue until you return to the original holes.

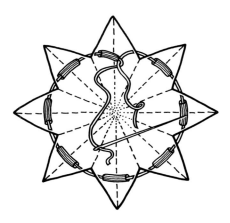

⑧ Remove the yarn from the needle. Holding one end of the yarn in each hand, pull the yarn until each of the noodle spacers are touching the paper on either side. Tie the yarn in a knot and trim off the ends.

THE STAR:

① Place tracing paper on top of figure D on page 51 and trace. Cut out tracing paper pattern. Place pattern on yellow construction paper and trace around it. Move pattern and trace around it again. Cut out both stars.

② Apply a thin, even layer of white liquid glue to one side of a star. Position the toothpick on the star as shown. Place the other star on top of the first star and line up the edges evenly. The toothpick will be sandwiched between the two stars. Set aside until glue sets.

3 Apply a thin, even layer of white liquid glue to one side of the star. Sprinkle with glitter. When glue has set, repeat on other side.

4 Tie two or three ribbons to the toothpick at the base of the star.

5 Slide the toothpick into the top of the tree.

TO DECORATE:

Our tree is decorated with ribbons and sequins attached with clear-drying glue. The garland is made of gold tinsel pipe cleaner strung with red beads. Use your imagination to come up with other decorating ideas.

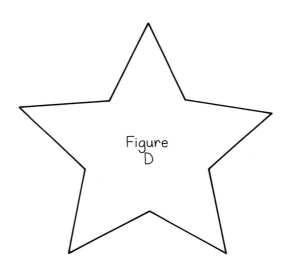

Figure D

Heavenly Feast

Celestial Seafood Casserole
▼
Tangy Mandarin Salad
▼
Starry Biscuits
▼
Chocolate Chip Pie on a Cloud
▼

Yuletide Angel

Celestial Seafood Casserole

YOU WILL NEED:

1 10½-ounce can cream of mushroom soup

1 cup milk

1 6-ounce can crab meat, drained

1 cup uncooked small macaroni shells

½ cup shredded cheddar cheese

2 tablespoons grated onion

¼ teaspoon dried parsley

1 Pour soup into casserole dish. Add milk, little by little, stirring after each addition.

2 Add remaining ingredients and stir well. Refrigerate overnight.

3 Preheat oven to 350°.

4 Bake casserole for 1 hour or until macaroni is tender.

Serves 4

Tangy Mandarin Salad

YOU WILL NEED:

1/4 head iceberg lettuce, torn into bite-size pieces

1/4 head romaine lettuce, torn into bite-size pieces

2 green onions, chopped

1 11-ounce can mandarin oranges, drained

1 cup chopped celery

1/4 cup shelled salted sunflower seeds

DRESSING:
2 tablespoons vinegar

1/4 cup vegetable oil

a few drops hot pepper sauce

1/2 teaspoon salt

2 tablespoons sugar

2 teaspoons dried parsley

1 In a large bowl, combine lettuce, onions, oranges, and celery. Toss gently with a fork.

2 Combine dressing ingredients in a bowl with a tight-fitting lid.

3 Cover bowl and shake until sugar is dissolved.

4 Pour dressing over salad. Sprinkle salad with sunflower seeds and serve.

Serves 4

Who Eats Eels for Christmas?

Here's a game that will make your mouth water. Try to match the Christmas foods with the country they come from. Then turn the book upside down to see how you did.

1. Denmark
2. England
3. France
4. Germany
5. Greece
6. Ireland
7. Italy
8. Poland
9. United States

A. roast pork, *baklava* (honey pastry)
B. roast goose, plum pudding
C. eels, *panettone* (Christmas bread)
D. knockwurst, red cabbage, gingerbread
E. baked ham, cranberries, sweet potatoes
F. spritz cookies, rice and almond pudding
G. potato pancakes, poppy seed cake
H. roast turkey, soda bread, mincemeat pie
I. *bûche de Noël* (log cake)

ANSWERS:
1F, 2B, 3I, 4D, 5A,
6H, 7C, 8G, 9E

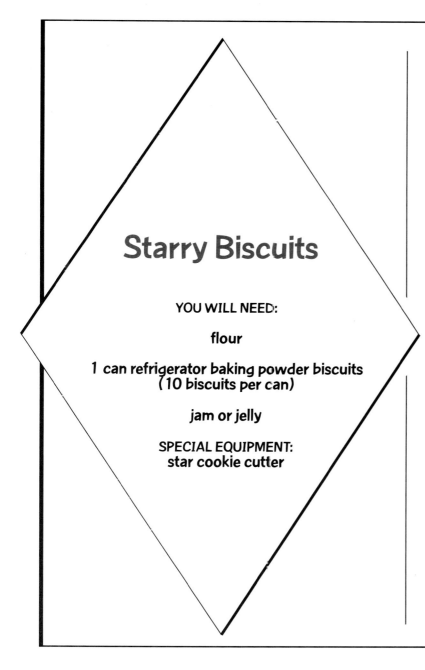

Starry Biscuits

YOU WILL NEED:

flour

1 can refrigerator baking powder biscuits (10 biscuits per can)

jam or jelly

**SPECIAL EQUIPMENT:
star cookie cutter**

① Preheat oven to temperature called for on biscuit package.

② Lay out a large piece of waxed paper. Dust waxed paper lightly with flour.

③ Separate biscuits and place on waxed paper. Dip cookie cutter in flour, and cut biscuits into star shapes. (If cookie cutter is slightly larger than biscuits, gently press the dough with the palm of your hand to make biscuits larger.)

④ Arrange biscuits on a baking sheet. Press your thumb into the center of each biscuit to make a hollow.

⑤ Use a teaspoon to fill hollows with jam.

⑥ Bake according to directions on biscuit package.

Makes 8 biscuits

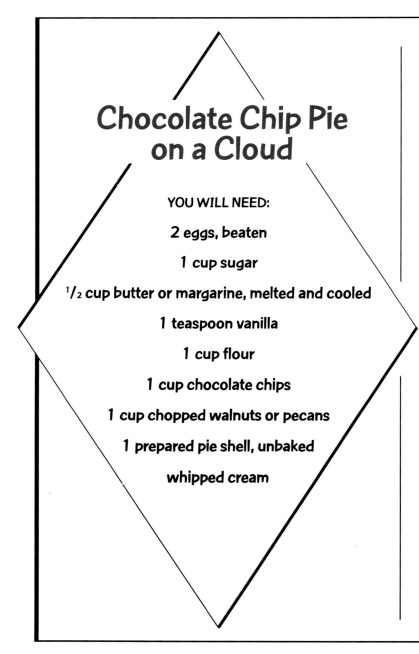

Chocolate Chip Pie on a Cloud

YOU WILL NEED:

2 eggs, beaten

1 cup sugar

$^1/_2$ cup butter or margarine, melted and cooled

1 teaspoon vanilla

1 cup flour

1 cup chocolate chips

1 cup chopped walnuts or pecans

1 prepared pie shell, unbaked

whipped cream

1 Preheat oven to 350°.

2 In a large bowl, combine beaten eggs, sugar, melted butter, and vanilla. Stir well.

3 Stir in flour.

4 Add chocolate chips and nuts and stir well.

5 Pour into pie shell.

6 Bake for 30 to 40 minutes or until a toothpick inserted in the center of pie comes out clean.

7 Serve with whipped cream.

Serves 6 to 8

Yuletide Angel

YOU WILL NEED:

pen

scissors

1 bowl, about 6 inches in diameter

1 7- by 7-inch piece of lace or netting

1 bead, ½ inch in diameter

2 gold tinsel pipe cleaners

5 inches of 1-inch wide satin ribbon

clear-drying glue (look for Super Tacky glue in sewing and craft stores)

❶ Place the bowl on top of the lace and trace around it with a pen. Be sure to place a piece of paper under the lace so you don't write on your working surface. Cut out the lace circle just inside the pen line.

❷ Place the bead on the fabric with the hole running straight up and down. Gather the lace around the bead. Wrap a pipe cleaner around the lace just under the bead as shown, and twist to secure. Do not trim the ends of the pipe cleaner.

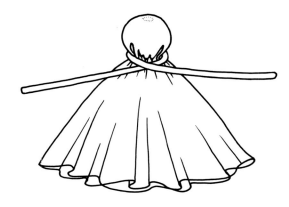

③ To make the wings, place the ribbon shiny side down in front of you. Loop one end around and glue it to the middle of the ribbon with clear-drying glue. Repeat with the other end of the ribbon. Hold the ends in place until the glue sets.

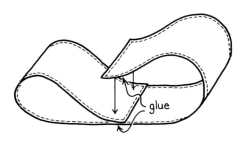

④ Pinch the wings together in the center and hold them just under the angel's head, on top of the pipe cleaner. Twist the pipe cleaner around the middle of the wings to attach them to the body. Trim the ends of the pipe cleaner.

⑤ To make the halo, wrap a pipe cleaner around a pencil to form a circle. Twist the pipe cleaner to secure it around the pencil. Slide the pencil out of the pipe cleaner circle. Trim off one end of the pipe cleaner right next to the circle. Trim off all but ½ inch of the other end of the pipe cleaner.

6 Apply clear-drying glue to the ½-inch section of pipe cleaner. Force the pipe cleaner through the fabric and into the hole in the top of the head. Wipe off any extra glue.

If you make several angels, you can make an angel mobile. Use white thread to attach the angels to a piece of pipe cleaner that has been twisted into a graceful shape.

O Christmas Tree

No one knows for sure who came up with the idea of bringing an evergreen tree inside and decorating it. But we do know that it was the Germans who made the idea into a popular Christmas tradition. Christmas trees became common in Germany in the 1600s. German Christmas trees were usually only four feet tall and they sat on tables. The trees were decorated with such things as apples, candies, and cookies. When the Christmas season was over, the ornaments would be shaken right off the tree so children could eat them. The Christmas tree tradition was brought to the United States by Germans who settled in Pennsylvania in the early 1800s. By the 1930s, Christmas trees were a common December sight across the country.

Recipe List

Beverages
    Chill-chasing Cider
    Cheery Hot Chocolate

Side Dishes
    Great Greeny Beanies
    Easy Elfin Rice
    Pear Mouse
    The Best Cinnamon Bread
    Tangy Mandarin Salad
    Starry Biscuits

Main Dishes
    Christmas Tree Tostada
    Crunchy Paprika Chicken
    Stroganoff St. Nick
    Ho-Ho-Holiday Omelet
    Celestial Seafood Casserole

Desserts
    Rudolph's Peanut Butter Oat Treats
    Chocolate-dipped Apple Slices
    Fantastic Fudge
        Frosty the Snowball
          Mrs. Claus's Favorite Lime Pie
           Chocolate Chip Pie on a Cloud

Glossary

beat—stir rapidly

Bundt pan—a pan used to make a round cake with a hole in the center

core—cut out the central part of a fruit, which often contains the seeds

crease—to run your fingers firmly along a fold so that the fold mark remains

drain—pour the liquid off of a food

dust—to cover with a light coating of a powdery substance, such as flour

fold—to mix by scooping up a substance with a spoon and turning it over on itself

grease—coat with a thin layer of butter, margarine, or shortening

green onion—a mild-flavored onion with a small bulb at one end and long, green leaves at the other

iceberg lettuce—a crisp, round lettuce with a very mild flavor

mandarin oranges—small, sweet oranges usually sold in cans

paper punch—a device used to punch small, round holes in paper

paprika—a red spice used as a seasoning and to give color to food

parsley—a green plant used as a garnish or to flavor food

pinking shears—scissors with serrated edges

pipe cleaner—a wire encased in fuzzy fabric

preheat—allow an oven to heat up to a certain temperature

romaine lettuce—lettuce with long, firm, light green leaves

score—to mark with a deep line or crease

sequin—a small, round, shiny piece of metal or plastic with a hole in the center

shred—cut into long, ragged pieces

sweetened condensed milk—milk with some of the water removed and sugar added

tortilla—a thin, round piece of bread made from corn or wheat flour

toss—combine foods by lightly lifting, turning, and dropping them with a fork

trace—copy a pattern onto another piece of paper

tracing paper—paper thin enough to be seen through when placed on top of a pattern

vanilla—a liquid used to give a vanilla flavor to foods

waxed paper—wax-coated paper often used in baking because food won't stick to it

Index

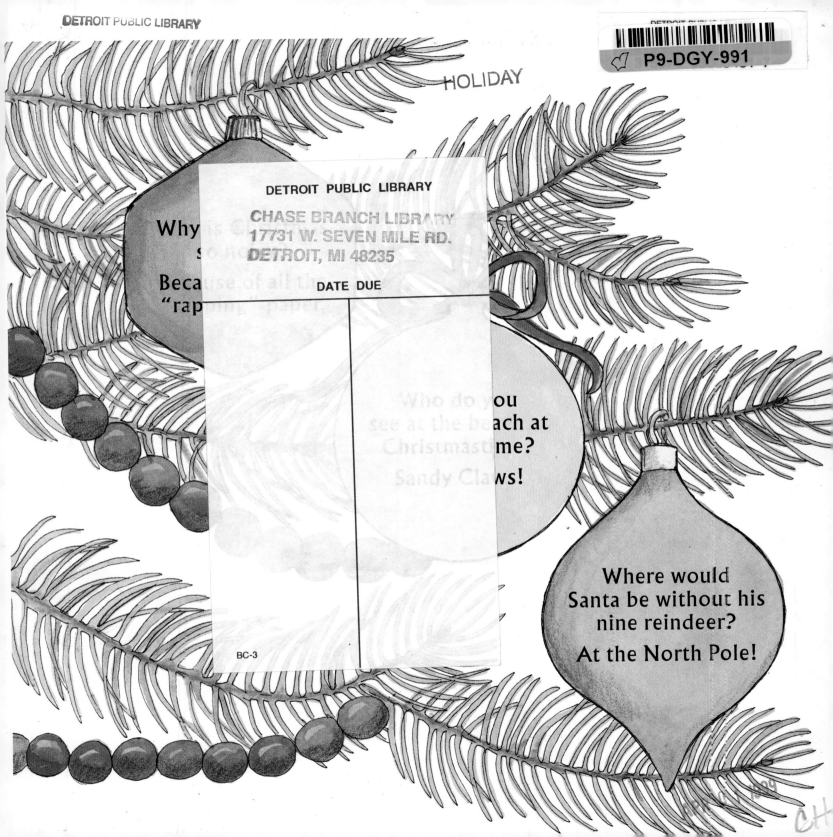

Why is Christmas paper
so loud?

Because of all the
"rapping" paper.

Who do you
see at the beach at
Christmastime?

Sandy Claws!

Where would
Santa be without his
nine reindeer?

At the North Pole!

LET'S CELEBRATE CHRISTMAS

by Peter and Connie Roop

Illustrated by
Katy Keck Arnsteen

The Millbrook Press
Brookfield, Connecticut

To Martha, whose joy of life gives all year long.
P. and C. Roop

For my SCBWI critique group,
always an inspiration.
K.K. Arnsteen

"The Night Before Christmas" was written by Clement C. Moore

Library of Congress Cataloging-in-Publication Data
Roop, Peter.
Let's celebrate Christmas / by Peter and Connie Roop;
illustrated by Katy Keck Arnsteen.
p. cm.
Summary: Presents some basic facts about Christmas, along with
jokes and riddles, Christmas crafts, and brief explanations of
Hanukkah and Kwanzaa.
ISBN 0-7613-0115-1 (lib. bdg.) ISBN 0-7613-0283-2 (pbk.)
1. Christmas—Juvenile literature. [1. Christmas.] I. Roop,
Connie. II. Arnsteen, Katy Keck, ill. III. Title.
GT4985.R66 1997 394.2663—dc21 97-4268 CIP AC

Published by The Millbrook Press
2 Old New Milford Road, Brookfield, CT 06804

Mexico	France	Italy	China

Feliz Navidad	Joyeux Noël	Buon Natale	Kung Hsi Hsin Nien

Poland		Germany
Wesolych Swiat		Fröhliche Weihnachten

MERRY CHRISTMAS from AROUND THE WORLD!

Japan		Ethiopia
Meri Kurisumasu		Melkm Ganna

South Africa	Sweden	Brazil	Holland

Een Plesierige Kerfees	Glad Jul	Boas Festas	Gelukkig Kerstfeest

WHY DO WE CELEBRATE CHRISTMAS?

Christmas Day is observed by Christians to celebrate the birth of Jesus. No one knows the exact day he was born, but in the year 349 Pope Julius I chose December 25 to be Jesus' birthday.

There was a good reason for this choice. Many festivals were already being held around this time to honor other gods. By linking Jesus' birth to these celebrations, the pope hoped people would also honor Jesus and become Christians.

One celebration was the Birthday of the Unconquered Sun. Because the winter sun wasn't as warm, and the days were shorter, people built huge fires on hills and mountaintops to give the sun strength. Although we no longer burn fires on hilltops, lights are everywhere at Christmastime—on trees, in windows, and decorating city streets.

WHO IS SANTA CLAUS?

Santa Claus was a real person named Nicholas.
Nicholas was a Christian bishop who lived in Asia Minor
long ago. Nicholas especially enjoyed giving treats to
poor children. He helped so many needy and poor people
that the Catholic Church made him a saint. Feasts were given
to honor Saint Nicholas's birthday on December 6.
Parents told their children Saint Nicholas would
give them presents if they were good.

In Holland, Dutch children put out their wooden shoes,
hoping Saint Nick would fill them with candy and treats. They
called him Sinter Klaas. Sinter Klaas did not come in a sleigh but
in a ship! Then he rode a white horse as he went from home to
home. Children put out carrots, water, and hay for Sinter
Klaas's horse. Sinter Klaas became our Santa Claus
when many Dutch people settled in America.

Santa is called Grandfather Frost in Russia. Presents are brought on Christmas Eve by an old woman named Babouschka.

In Japan, Santa is called Hoteiosho. He has eyes in the back of his head to watch for good children. He gives gifts out of his pack.

In Sweden children wait for Jultomten at Christmas.

WHY DOES SANTA COME DOWN THE CHIMNEY?

People long ago believed in a goddess named Hertha. Hertha watched over their homes. She protected them from illness. As winter began, families had a special feast to honor Hertha. They built huge fires in their fireplaces. Hertha would come down the chimney through the smoke to give them good luck for the next year. Our word "hearth" comes from Hertha.

These early beliefs about Hertha are thought to be the reason why we believe our Santa Claus comes down the chimney. Santa, however, doesn't bring us good luck. Instead he brings us presents for being good the past year. Even if you don't have a chimney, Santa will find you if you have been good.

In Sweden, Jultomten arrives in a sleigh pulled by a goat.

In Mexico, the Three Kings bring gifts and the children leave straw out for the kings' camels.

In Ghana, the children believe that Father Christmas comes from the jungle.

In a part of Australia, a white-bearded Santa wearing a red bathing suit arrives on water skis.

In China, Lan Khoong-Khoong (Nice Old Father) brings presents to children's stockings.

WHY DO WE GIVE PRESENTS AT CHRISTMAS?

Gift-giving in December is an old custom. At the ancient December festivals people gave gifts of candles, lamps, and evergreens to their friends and families. Others gave money to help the poor.

In the Bible story, Joseph and Mary go to an inn but there is no room for them. They are sent to the stable, and that night Jesus is born. He is laid in a manger with animals all around. Overhead a bright star shines, showing the way to the Three Kings who come to see the new baby, bringing precious gifts of gold, frankincense, and myrrh. Myrrh and frankincense are sweet-smelling gums used in perfumes. Gold meant that someday Jesus would be a king. Frankincense meant he would be a high priest. Myrrh, also used in embalming, foretold his death.

SAINT NICHOLAS' DAY
DECEMBER 6

People in
Belgium and
Holland exchange
gifts on this day.

SAINT STEPHEN'S DAY
DECEMBER 26

This is also known
as Boxing Day
in England,
because of all the
Christmas boxes.

ST. LUCIA'S DAY
DECEMBER 13

This is the
gift-giving day
in Sweden.

EPIPHANY
JANUARY 6

Many Catholic
countries give
gifts to celebrate
the Epiphany.

WHY DO WE HANG STOCKINGS AT CHRISTMAS?

A special Christmas tradition is hanging your stocking for Santa to fill with small presents. This tradition comes to us from Holland, where children hang stockings for Sinter Klaas to fill.

But why stockings? Here is one story. Long ago there was a merchant who had three daughters. Sadly, the merchant somehow lost all of his money. His daughters were going to be sold as servants to pay his bills. During their last night at home the girls washed their stockings and hung them by the fire to dry. Bishop Nicholas, hearing about their fate, dropped gold down the chimney into each girl's stocking. The girls were saved! When their father heard who had given the gold, he went around town praising Bishop Nicholas.

Ever since, children have hung stockings by the chimney in the hopes that Santa Claus will fill their stockings with gifts, too.

WHAT IS A CRÈCHE?

A crèche is a manger scene showing Mary, Joseph, and the baby Jesus. Most often the animals who would have been in the stable are also shown. The scene was first created in 1224 by Saint Francis in Italy. He used real people and animals. Today we have wooden or plastic people and animals to re-create the Nativity scene.

WHY DO WE DECORATE TREES?

Legend has it that a German man named Martin
Luther went walking in the woods on a starry Christmas Eve.
Starlight twinkled on the snowy branches of the fir trees.
Martin Luther cut down a fir tree, took it home, and decorated
it with candles so that it twinkled like the sparkling trees
in the forest. People enjoyed his tree so much,
they wanted one for themselves.

The first Christmas trees were small—often just
the tops of taller trees. The idea of bringing in a tall tree
stretching from floor to ceiling began later in America.

The first decorations were apples, paper roses,
cookies, candy, and candles. Later, nuts, gingerbread,
toys, dolls, oranges, glass icicles, and balls and
other ornaments were added.

Not all trees were decorated with expensive
ornaments. Many pioneer children decorated their trees
with pinecones, seed pods, strings of popcorn and
cranberries, and other natural ornaments. Farm children
often made gingerbread ornaments in the shapes of
animals. Fat hogs, hopping rabbits, and galloping
horses hung on many family Christmas trees.

A star is often placed at the top of the Christmas tree. This star represents the star shining over Bethlehem when Jesus was born. Some families place paper or glass angels on their treetops.

Early Christmas trees were beautiful with their ornaments and glittering candles. But having lighted candles on a tree was dangerous. The tree might catch fire. About a hundred years ago Thomas Edison invented the electric lightbulb. One of his friends put some of Edison's lights on his Christmas tree. With electric lights people could enjoy a lighted Christmas tree and worry less about fire. Since then, trees inside and outside have been shining brilliantly at Christmastime.

President Teddy Roosevelt did not want people cutting down trees, so he did not allow a Christmas tree in the White House. His two sons, however, smuggled a tree into their closet.

The General Grant Tree in California is our national Christmas Tree. This giant sequoia is 267 feet tall and is over 3,500 years old.

Old Christmas trees are used for lining snowmobile paths, sunk in lakes to make homes for fish, or ground up to make chips for hiking trails.

Christmas trees are grown in all fifty states, including Hawaii!

WHY DO WE SING CAROLS AT CHRISTMAS?

The first Christmas carols were dance tunes, not Christmas songs. Long ago in Greece, a "carol" was a ring of dancers who danced to flute music. The men and women dancers formed a chain holding hands as they danced.

Carol dancing was such fun that it became part of many Christmas festivities. In many Spanish-speaking countries, dancing and singing are a Christmas highlight.

Christmas music is a wonderful part of the season.
Many popular carols, like "Silent Night" and "Hark! The Herald
Angels Sing," came from Europe. "O Little Town
of Bethlehem" and "We Three Kings of Orient Are" were written
in America especially for children.

In America, going from house to house singing carols
is popular. Swedish children sing carols and dance with their
parents around the family Christmas tree. In France carols
are often sung during Christmas plays and pageants. In Wales
many carols are sung to gentle music of a harp. In Puerto Rico,
carolers ride on horseback, singing their songs to music
of guitars and maracas. All around the world, music
is a special part of the Christmas season.

WHAT KINDS OF FOOD DO PEOPLE EAT ON CHRISTMAS?

Most families have traditional dishes that they like to serve every year. Some of the dishes described on this page are only made for Christmas because they are richer and more difficult to make.

Bûche de Noël is a rich chocolate cake from France made to look like a Yule log.

In Sweden they make pepparkakor—Christmas gingersnaps.

Plum pudding from England contains no plums and is not a pudding but a delicious cake.

Stollen and Lebkuchen are treats from Germany studded with candied fruits.

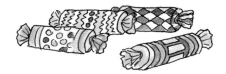

In England the Christmas dinner table is set with crackers, hollow paper tubes filled with candies or small goodies.

Christmas cookies in America are shaped like trees and wreaths and are often made and decorated by the whole family.

Kourabiedes from Greece are cookies that each have a clove, to symbolize the spices brought to Jesus by the Three Kings.

Panettone is a sweet raisin and chestnut-studded holiday bread from Italy.

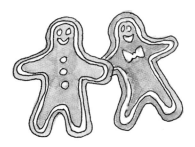

Gingerbread has been a holiday treat since the 14th century. It is used to make gingerbread men and enchanting gingerbread houses.

DO SOME OF YOUR FRIENDS CELEBRATE HANUKKAH?

Long ago Jewish people held a special festival in December that continues today. This celebration is called Hanukkah, or the Feast of Lights. Hanukkah is celebrated in honor of the Lord saving the Jews from their enemies.

Hanukkah lasts for eight days. A candlestick called a menorah is put in a special place in the home. Each day a new candle is lit until all eight are burning brightly. Gifts wrapped in blue and white paper are exchanged. Fried potato pancakes called latkes are served with sour cream and applesauce. Playing games is a fun part of Hanukkah. One game is spinning the dreidel, a four-sided top. Each side has a letter on it. You win candy or coins or nothing depending on which letter lands up.

Make a Menorah Banner

Materials: Four pieces of 9 x 12 in. felt
(1 white, 1 yellow, 2 blue)
glue
scissors
ruler

  1. Place the two pieces of blue felt together along the 12-in. side as pictured.

2. Cut two 1 ½ x 12 in. strips from the yellow felt and glue one of them over the seam of the two blue pieces to join them together.

 3. Cut the other yellow strip into two sizes: 6 x 1 ½ in. and 5 x 1 ½ in. Center the 6-in. strip vertically and the 5-in. strip horizontally on the bottom, as pictured, and glue.

 4. Take the rest of the yellow felt and cut it in half for a 6 x 6 in. square. Cut this diagonally from corner to corner to form two triangles.

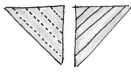 5. Measure and cut the triangles into five ¾-in. wide strips.

 6. Arrange the four smallest pieces as shown in the picture. Do both sides, leaving some blue showing in between. Glue.

 7. Cut eight white strips, each 1 x 4 ½ in. for the candles, and one strip 1 x 5 ½ in. Put the longest in the center and evenly space the rest on the yellow center strip.

 8. Using the last two ¾-in. wide yellow strips, cut nine diamond shapes for the candle flames. Glue down center flame. Tack to wall or make loops from leftover felt to hang.

 9. Add a new flame on a candle for each day of Hanukkah.

DO SOME OF YOUR FRIENDS CELEBRATE KWANZAA?

Kwanzaa is a special African-American celebration that lasts seven days. Kwanzaa begins on December 26 and runs through January 1. Kwanzaa is rooted in African harvest festivals called First Fruits. These harvest celebrations have been shared throughout Africa for hundreds of years. The days for Kwanzaa match the times First Fruits are celebrated in Africa.

There are seven principles honored during Kwanzaa, each highlighted with its own candle in a kinara, or candleholder. Each day a new principle is celebrated and a new candle lit.

The principles are Umoja (unity), Kujichagulia (self-determination), Ujima (working together and responsibility), Ujamaa (cooperative economics), Nia (purpose), Kuumba (creativity), and Imani (faith). During Kwanzaa, families come together, gifts are shared, and thanks are given.

Dr. Maulana Karenga created Kwanzaa in 1966 for African Americans to honor their ancestors and their traditions.

MAKE A MKEKA, THE KWANZAA PLACEMAT

Here is what you need:

large sheets of red, black, and green construction paper,
scissors, glue, and a ruler.

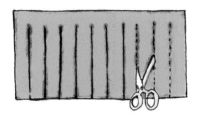

1. Measure 1 in. down from the long edge of your paper. Then cut 1-in. strips vertically to that line.

2. Cut the other 2 pieces of paper into 1-in. strips the long way.

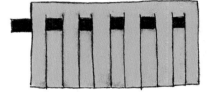

3. Weave one strip under and over the vertical cuts until you get to the end.

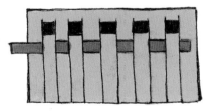

4. Weave the second strip of a different color by going over and under.

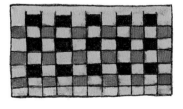

5. Continue weaving until you run out of room. Glue the ends down so they will not slip out.

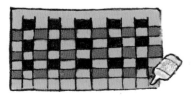

6. You can glue a card to the back of your placemat explaining the colors: Red is for the struggle to be free, black is for unity, and green is for a better future.

IT IS JUST AS NICE TO GIVE AS IT IS TO RECEIVE!

Some of the best gifts are the ones you make yourself!

OLD-FASHIONED CLOVED FRUIT. You will need: Oranges and lemons, cloves, thimble. Push the slender end of the cloves into the fruit in a pretty pattern. You don't have to cover the whole fruit, although you could. Put a thimble on your thumb to help push the cloves in. Pin a loop of ribbon to the top of the fruit so it can hang, or put two or three decorated fruits in a bowl.

PICTURE ORNAMENT. You will need: Christmas card or your drawing of a Christmas tree, pictures of yourself and your family, cardboard, string. Draw a Christmas tree, or cut one out of an old Christmas card. Carefully cut out round spaces to look like ornaments and tape pictures of yourself and your family so your faces show through the holes. Glue the tree onto a cardboard backing. Tape a string onto the frame, and friends and family can enjoy you hanging around every Christmas!

PINECONE BIRD FEEDER. You will need: Pinecone, yarn, peanut butter, birdseed. Take a pinecone and tie a piece of strong yarn around the base. Cover the pinecone with peanut butter. Roll the pinecone in birdseed and hang it from a branch outside. You can put more peanut butter and seeds on the cone when the birds have finished. Try different seeds to see what they like.

BARRETTE HOLDER. You will need: Yarn, ribbon, glue. Make a thick 12-in. braid of different-colored pieces of yarn. Decorate with a ribbon bow on the top and bottom. Attach a loop to the top.

NO-MESS MESSAGE BOARD. You will need: Cardboard, big colored rubber bands, 24-in. string, glue. Cut four pieces of cardboard, each measuring 9 x 9 in. Glue the first two pieces together and then glue the other two pieces together. Now position the string so that 3 in. on both ends are on the cardboard. Glue the two double pieces of cardboard together with the string in between. When the glue has dried, cover the board with crisscrossing rubber bands. Keep adding rubber bands until you are happy with the way it looks. Use at least ten rubber bands. Decorate with stickers or leave it plain. Tuck a new pencil and some scrap paper under a rubber band.

MAKE A CHRISTMAS GARLAND

There are lots of different kinds of garlands you can make, and lots of places to put them. Think about decorating the Christmas tree, doorways, and mantlepieces.

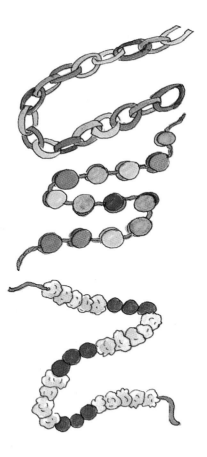

CHRISTMAS RINGS: Cut colored construction paper into strips 1/2 in. to 1 in. wide. With your first strip tape the ends together to make a ring. Take the second strip and run it through the first ring before taping the ends together. You can make all the rings the same size, or you can make them all different sizes, or try one big ring then one small, etc.

CIRCLE STRINGS: Cut a long piece of yarn. Then cut out 1-in. circles from colored papers. Paste two circles together with the yarn centered in between, and as you paste try to leave the same amount of yarn between the circles. Decorate the circles with glued-on glitter, felt pens, or tin foil.

POPCORN AND CRANBERRY ROPE: Thread a long sturdy needle with heavy-duty thread. Run the needle through five or six pieces of popcorn and then two or three cranberries. Leave plenty of thread at each end because you will have to tie your rope together to make one long garland. This garland can go outside to wish the birds a Merry Christmas!

WRAP IT UP!

Make your own wrapping paper!

The funny papers make great wrapping paper. Finish it off with brightly colored yarn or ribbon.

Open up a grocery bag so that it lies flat. Decorate with pictures from old Christmas cards, glitter, felt-tipped pens, glued swirls of yarn, or wrapped hard candies, glued on. Or leave the paper plain and top off your package with small pine branches knotted in the ribbon.

Small lunch bags or bakery bags are perfect for odd-shaped presents. Decorate the bag with some of the ideas described above. Punch holes along the top and weave in ribbon or yarn for a drawstring.

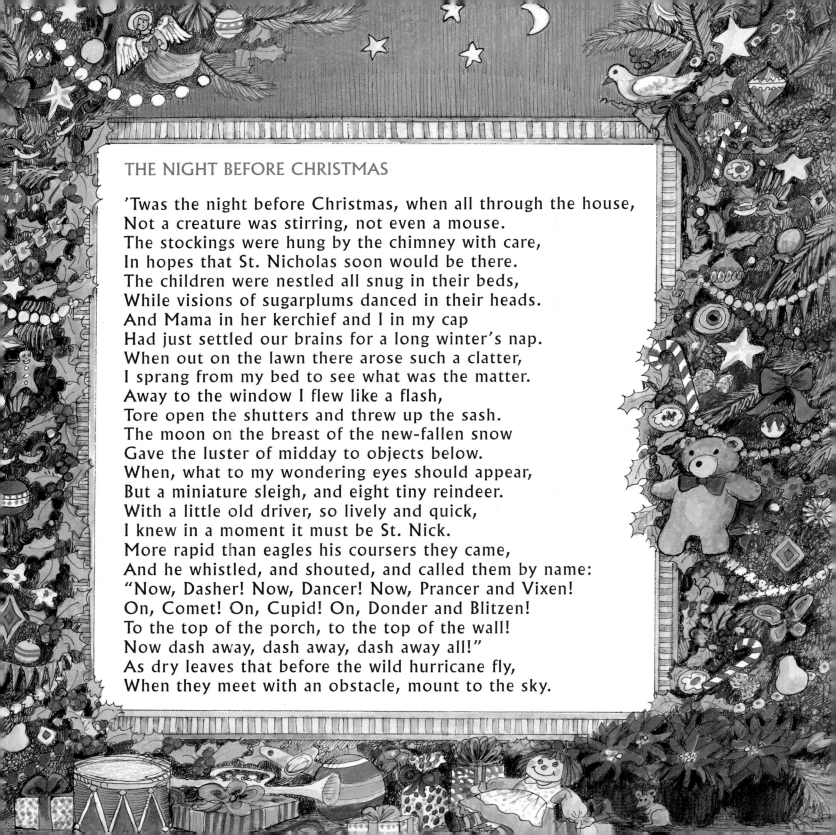

THE NIGHT BEFORE CHRISTMAS

'Twas the night before Christmas, when all through the house,
Not a creature was stirring, not even a mouse.
The stockings were hung by the chimney with care,
In hopes that St. Nicholas soon would be there.
The children were nestled all snug in their beds,
While visions of sugarplums danced in their heads.
And Mama in her kerchief and I in my cap
Had just settled our brains for a long winter's nap.
When out on the lawn there arose such a clatter,
I sprang from my bed to see what was the matter.
Away to the window I flew like a flash,
Tore open the shutters and threw up the sash.
The moon on the breast of the new-fallen snow
Gave the luster of midday to objects below.
When, what to my wondering eyes should appear,
But a miniature sleigh, and eight tiny reindeer.
With a little old driver, so lively and quick,
I knew in a moment it must be St. Nick.
More rapid than eagles his coursers they came,
And he whistled, and shouted, and called them by name:
"Now, Dasher! Now, Dancer! Now, Prancer and Vixen!
On, Comet! On, Cupid! On, Donder and Blitzen!
To the top of the porch, to the top of the wall!
Now dash away, dash away, dash away all!"
As dry leaves that before the wild hurricane fly,
When they meet with an obstacle, mount to the sky.

So up to the housetop the coursers they flew,
With a sleigh full of toys, and St. Nicholas, too!
And then in a twinkling, I heard on the roof,
The prancing and pawing of each little hoof.
As I drew in my head, and was turning around,
Down the chimney St. Nicholas came with a bound.
He was dressed all in fur, from his head to his foot,
And his clothes were all tarnished with ashes and soot.
A bundle of toys he had flung on his back,
And he looked like a peddler just opening his pack.
His eyes how they twinkled! His dimples how merry!
His cheeks were like roses, his nose like a cherry.
His droll little mouth was drawn up like a bow,
And the beard on his chin was as white as the snow.
The stump of a pipe he held tight in his teeth,
And the smoke, it encircled his head like a wreath.
He had a broad face and a little round belly
That shook, when he laughed, like a bowl full of jelly.
He was chubby and plump, a right jolly old elf,
And I laughed when I saw him in spite of myself.
A wink of his eye, and a twist of his head,
Soon gave me to know I had nothing to dread.
He spoke not a word, but went straight to his work,
And filled all the stockings, then turned with a jerk.
And laying his finger aside of his nose,
And giving a nod, up the chimney he rose.
He sprang to his sleigh, to his team gave a whistle,
And away they all flew like the down of a thistle.
But I heard him exclaim, ere he drove out of sight,
"HAPPY CHRISTMAS TO ALL, AND TO ALL A GOOD NIGHT!"

ABOUT THE AUTHORS

Connie and Peter Roop have been making and giving presents all their lives. Both are teachers who share the gift of their knowledge with children every day of the year. The authors of twenty-five books, they also share their love of reading and writing with children across America. They are the parents of Sterling and Heidi, who share their gifts of love and friendship around Appleton, Wisconsin, and in the many places to which the Roop family travels.

ABOUT THE ILLUSTRATOR

Katy Keck Arnsteen has illustrated over forty books for children. Her background in fine arts and teaching combines for bright illustrations.